THE CHRISTMAS GOSPELS

Ever Upward,

THE CHRISTMAS GOSPELS
2017. Jason Korsiak

This is a book of crititcal essays based on motion pictures and isn't authorized by any studio or production company. These essays are the opinion of the author and make no assumptions about the spirituality or the intent of the filmmakers involved with the movies addressed herein.

Portions of this book contain the recounting of personal experiences. The author has attempted to accurately recollect events to the best of his ability and has intentionally altered the names and characteristics of certain persons out of respect for their privacy.

Scripture quotations taken from the Holy Bible, New International Version®, NIV®. Copyright ©1973, 1978, 1984, 2011 by Biblica, Inc.™ Used by permission of Zondervan. All rights reserved worldwide. www.zondervan.com The "NIV" and "New International Version" are trademarks registered in the United States Patent and Trademark Office by Biblica, Inc.™

ISBN-13: 978-1541090484   ISBN-10: 1541090489

Cover photography and design by Brian Trumble.
Edited by Jason Korsiak and Brian Trumble.
Author photo by Jodie Griggs.

This work is dedicated to Aunt Joan, my godmother, for the simple gift of a VHS of holiday cartoons that unknowingly set me on a path to faith and to writing this book.

In memory of David Huddleston
(1930 – 2016)
Thank you, Santa.

~ CONTENTS ~

"Christmas is a season not only of
rejoicing but also reflecting."

Winston Churchill

THE CHRISTMAS GOSPELS

Jason Korsiak

~ AN ~
INTRODUCTION

"He who has not Christmas in his heart will never find it under a tree."

Roy L. Smith

One of the most precious gifts that I was ever given is a plush bear that I named Bee Bee. The story goes that my parents left me with my godmother one evening when I was about two so that they could go to a concert. It was an Amy Grant concert, I think, and, if I'm not mistaken, it was their first night out together after I was born. I have no memory of it myself, of course, but I was told that Bee Bee was in my

1

crib when my parents came back to pick me up and that nobody knew where he came from. Obviously, that wasn't true; Bee Bee was just a loving gift from my family, but as a child I believed the story whole-heartedly. I speculated over whether Bee Bee was a gift from a guardian angel or if he was perhaps just an early present from Santa. Either way, Bee Bee was special to me and was especially loved.

I brought Bee Bee everywhere. One time when I was maybe four I accidentally left him at a department store that my family would frequent on the boulevard where I grew up in Queens. I didn't realize that he was gone until a kind, old lady came rushing out to stop us (reinforcing that guardian angel theory). I played too roughly with him at a different store and the thread attaching his arm to his body gave way.

"His arm fell off!" I howled with all the urgency of someone who had seen somebody get dismembered. The girl at the counter whirled around as if looking for a leper.

"Who!? Who?!" she shrieked in horror. Then, she saw me there with woeful eyes holding up a stuffed bear. She and my parents had a pretty good laugh.

Another gift I received at my godmother's house was a VHS tape of Christmas cartoons. Hidden inside the Pepto-Bismol pink box was an assortment of public domain shorts from the 1950's. Most of them were made by Castle Films, like a live action version of *A Visit from Saint Nick* and an animated battle between a tin soldier and a jack-in-the-box over some Little Bo Peep damsel under the tree. My favorite short was about a king who snuck two hobos into his castle after meeting Santa at a toy store. I seldom made it past the first few shorts before falling asleep and never saw the last one on the cassette. In fact, the first time I ever saw it was Christmas Eve 1989, which was our first in Florida.

I was homesick for my grandma, for my aunt, and for snow. I was also worried about Bee Bee. My mother was always ready with the thread to patch up the war wounds of his various adventures; but there was only so much anyone could do to repair one small bear. Unbeknownst to me, my parents found another "Bee Bee," but told me to pray that he would be fixed. Now, I had gone to Catholic School. I knew the Rosary, and the lesson that the priest would give when he visited us was always the highlight of my school week (despite church not being a part of my upbringing), yet praying was largely alien to me. Certainly, if I did pray, I didn't understand Who or What exactly I was praying to.

I couldn't sleep. Part of it, no doubt, was because of my enthusiasm for Christmas morning, but mainly it was

3

because it was the very first night since I had been given Bee Bee that he wasn't with me. Lying awake, I did the one thing that I'd never done before: watched to the end of the VHS. The short was a marionette version of the Christmas story. We had a nativity - a beautiful ceramic one my mother had painted - but I didn't understand who the figurines were or what they were doing there. Don't get me wrong, the short wasn't that great. It was almost dream-like; the marionettes moved like they were under water and the narration was so monotonous that it's any wonder it didn't put me to sleep then. But it was the message, rather than the content of the short, that captivated me. I grasped, insofar as a seven year old *can* grasp, anyway, God and what the birth of Christ meant. That night, I prayed understanding who Jesus is and consider that night, alone and with no one's input, to be the night that I became a Christian. To my astonishment, I was greeted the next morning by my beloved Bee Bee, restored - a present from "Santa" and the answer to my first fervent prayer.

Were my parents cheating a bit? Maybe. They had me pray knowing already that my hope would be fulfilled. Still, anyone who ever got their first bike on Christmas morning knows that the training wheels are only there to introduce us to that new mode of travel. Eventually, we can journey by ourselves. Christmas is like the training wheels of faith, introducing us to a new mode of thinking, the goal of which is ultimately traveling with God ourselves.

Holiday specials teach us a lot about belief. Some Christians recoil at the image of Santa or of flying reindeer, but I believe that these stories can be used for wonderful lessons and that we can grow as families and as individuals when we gather around the hearth of our televisions to share in their fantasy.

I love Christmas, and holiday cartoons and specials have remained a major part of my season each year. Whether it's the clunky stop motion of Rankin/Bass classics like *The Year Without a Santa Claus* or polished films like *Arthur Christmas* and *Miracle on 34th Street*, I enjoy them all. Even movies that aren't *technically* Christmas movies but have a strong Christmas-bent, such as *Gremlins*, have a place in my heart. As a Christian who is often very busy trying to juggle my time around Christmas between church expectations and obligations to friends or family, I decided to build an entire devotional around holiday specials. We watch them anyway, so why not also get a little more out of them, too?

If you also love these stories and struggle to balance

your sacred and secular sides at Christmas, then this book is for you. Each chapter has suggested verses and questions for your journal. These reflections are spoiler-heavy and presume that you've seen the films in question, so I recommend that you watch them first. If you don't want to watch them, or can't, each chapter has enough plot summary to understand the devotion. Also, even though every film in this book is either PG or lower, each chapter includes rating information to guide your viewing schedule. That said, I would caution against sharing this with young readers; it's written for those who "know the truth" about a certain, red-suited Christmas legend. Of course, this book isn't for every believer. Some Christians will always reject the legend, but a stuffed bear from Santa once showed me that the most fantastic legends can reveal the most profound truths.

~ 1 ~
THE NIGHTMARE BEFORE CHRISTMAS

"Just because I cannot see it doesn't mean
I can't believe it!"

Year: 1993
Distributor: Buena Vista Pictures
Producers: Tim Burton, Denise DiNovi
Director: Henry Selick
Writer: Caroline Thompson from an adaptation by Michael McDowell, based on characters created by Tim Burton
Runtime: 76 minutes
Rating: PG

Scripture Reading: 1 Timothy 3:1-7

The progenitor of macabre stop-motion films like *Coraline* and *Frankenweenie* (which itself was an adaption of creator Tim Burton's earlier work), *The Nightmare Before Christmas* began as a poem written by Burton during his tenure at Disney. The film wasn't directed by him, however, but was directed by Henry Selick, who crafted a timeless special that straddles two holidays and went on to become a pop culture phenomenon.

The film creates a unique universe in which all of the holidays exist in their own pocket realities, like towns. A long, woeful walk through the woods leads Jack Skellington, the disenfranchised king of Halloween Town, to a circle of trees with doors shaped like holiday symbols. Jack is drawn to the doorway of Christmas Town, a Seussian wonderland of joy and color. Christmas Town takes a hold of Jack's heart immediately, and, like a new convert, he can't wait to share his experience with everyone. He calls a town meeting where he tries to explain Christmas to the denizens of Halloween Town, but they struggle to understand, so, perched at his pulpit like a twisted preacher, Jack warps Christmas into a darker interpretation that his fellow haunts might fathom.

Squirreling himself away in his tower for days and conducting weird experiments on Christmas bric-a-brac in the hopes of scientifically deducing what makes Christmas special, Jack finally sees the light: Christmas isn't something that can be logically figured out, only *experienced.*

Sadly, Jack's enthusiasm goes too far and he plots to take over Christmas for himself. Calamity ensues as Jack's 'elves,' the people of Halloween Town, try to make gifts for the world's children, not realizing how inappropriate the horrors they're concocting are. In all of the town, there is only one person who attempts to reason with Jack, a rag doll named Sally who is secretly in love with him. Sally has a terrible vision of Jack's Christmas plans going up in flames (which they do), but he shoos her away.

The distinction between Jack and Sally is fascinating. Both are lonely, but for different reasons. Sally is lonely because she was created, not unlike Frankenstein's monster, by a scientist who keeps her locked away for himself. Jack is lonely because everyone in town is too busy idolizing him to realize that he needs help out of his rut. He is adored by all, but only Sally seems to truly appreciate and challenge him. Everybody could use a Sally.

Jack weaves a popcorn chain of disaster wherever his skeleton reindeer carry him. The crisis is so urgent that the military shoots him down, landing him in a graveyard where he bemoans that he's spoiled Christmas just because he wasn't content as the Pumpkin King.

A lot of us try to become leaders in arenas where we might not be qualified. Our scripture today describes the standards for someone who would be a church leader. Often, we associate this passage with pastors, but it applies to any church leader, paid or not. One of the most important (and tragically overlooked) items on the list is that the potential new leader should *not* be a recent convert. Why? Because, as with Jack, the hubris of new faith is dazzling to others on the outside, but it can make one proud and self-centered. Like many new believers who want to go out and be pastors, Jack isn't content to just celebrate Christmas and apply his refreshed enthusiasm to the position he already has; rather, he thinks that he can do better than Santa. Recall what Verse 6 in our passage says about the new convert who's allowed to become a leader: they can find themselves sitting in the same seat of judgment as the devil. What was his sin? Believing he could run things better than God.

The film ends with Santa bringing Christmas magic to Halloween, showing that he forgives Jack. This marriage of the two holidays reminds me that no two Christians are alike. There are numberless ways to celebrate Jesus, and, just like the townspeople of Halloween have their own distinct traditions, the church is big enough for all of us to honor God in our own way without taking it over.

JOURNAL QUESTIONS
- Have you ever been tempted to "take over" something?
- What unique traditions do you or your family have that makes Christmas special for you?

~ 2 ~
MIRACLE ON 34ᵗʰ STREET

"Faith is believing when common sense tells you not to. Don't you see? It's not just Kris that's on trial, it's everything he stands for. It's kindness and joy and love and all the other intangibles."

Year: 1947
Distributor: 20ᵗʰ Century Fox
Producer: William Perlberg
Director: George Seaton
Writer: George Season, based on a story by Valentine Davies
Runtime: 96 minutes
Rating: Approved

Scripture Reading: John 18:28-40

I have a confession to make. I never saw today's film until working on this book, and I feel robbed! *Miracle on 34ᵗʰ Street* deserves all the praise it receives. Though the film technically stars Maureen O'Hara and John Payne, the story centers around Edmund Gwenn as Kris Kringle and Natalie Wood as Susan, a serious-minded little girl whom he's trying to win over while proving that he is, indeed, Santa Claus.

The film opens with the Macy's Thanksgiving Parade getting ready to kick off when Gwenn discovers its Santa is drunk. Filling in as a last minute replacement, he becomes the highlight of the parade and is asked to be Macy's official store Santa for the holiday shopping season. Susan's mother, Doris (O'Hara), is his boss, and the only thing she has less time for than imagination are the advances of her neighbor, Fred Gailey (Payne), a lawyer who is smitten with her.

Although Kris charms everyone he meets, concern is raised when it's discovered that he believes himself to be the *real* Santa. After lashing out at the store psychologist, Kris is put in a mental hospital. Coming to his aid, Gailey chooses to represent him in court and not only prove his innocence but also his claim that he *is* Father Christmas.

One of the movie's great strengths is balancing the multiple plots and finding a through-line. It's not just about Kris proving himself, it's about Doris and Susan coming to belief. It's about Gailey as a lovelorn man trying to win the woman he adores. It's about the power of generosity winning over corporate agendas. It's about a boy who's been made to feel ashamed of himself for wanting to play Santa for kids. It's about a judge struggling to do right for his career as well as his conscience.

Additionally commendable is the movie's choice to keep the film grounded in reality. We see no miracles on 34th Street, just the warmth of someone who could both be Santa or just be a well-intended old man with a delusion. There are no magical displays, nor are there elves or other trappings of the legend. In fact, were I to lobby any complaint about the movie it would be that, for a story about a court hearing trying to prove whether or not Santa is real, you'd think that some of the fantastic aspects of the mythos would come up. There's no talk of the North Pole or flying reindeer. That's one thing I would credit the 1994 remake for doing better.

One of the more unique aspects of *Miracle on 34th Street* is how it was released and marketed. The trailer, which is just a studio executive talking to actors around the 20th Century Fox lot about how great the film is, doesn't say anything about it being a Christmas movie. Why? Because it debuted in May, less than a month after Easter that year. The gamble paid off, making *Miracle on 34th Street* one of the biggest hits of 1947. It strikes me that *Miracle on 34th Street* might have performed better still had it come out a little sooner, because, in spite of being about Christmas, it's a perfect Easter movie.

Consider the character of Judge Harper; he wants to

do his job fairly but the pressure of such a high profile case, one which speaks to intangible matters of belief, puts him in a very awkward position. The man before him claims to be Santa Claus, but everyone knows that's impossible. Even his political adviser, Charlie, warns that taking the case could be career suicide, comparing him to Pontius Pilate, a governor who found himself in a similar predicament with a man who claimed to be the Son of God. Neither defendant can prove nor disprove his claims, and both "judges" eagerly want a way out of the position that they've been put in.

It is the belief of the masses which sways each 'judge'. Pilate condemns Christ on the whim of the angry throng, but it's the faith of the world's children that moves Judge Harper to exonerate Kris. What connects the two is that they each wanted an out. The world is filled with Judge Harpers, looking for others to confirm their faith or their disbelief. The question is which crowd do our choices reflect in our mission to sway them?

JOURNAL QUESTIONS
- How do our actions silently persuade others?
- What's been the most effective way to "win someone over" in your life?

~ 3 ~
ERNEST SAVES CHRISTMAS

"You know, I've carried this torch for more
seasons than I should have done, because I
loved it so much."

Year: 1988
Distributor: Buena Vista Pictures
Producer: Joseph Akerman
Director: John R. Cherry III
Writers: B. Cline, Ed Turner
Runtime: 95 minutes
Rating: PG

Scripture Reading: 1 Corinthians 7:26-35

Ernest P. Worrell, the signature character of the late
Jim Varney, was a spokesman for hire created by ad agency
Carden & Cherry. He was licensed out to a number of local
and national companies, appearing in commercials for just
about anything from Sprite to Mellow Yellow, Purity Milk to
Pontiac. The genius of the ads was that the setups were basic
enough to swap out the products and use the same sketch
for multiple clients. Ernest was so popular that he was able

to transition to the big screen. In this film, Ernest is a down and out cab driver whose passenger is none other than Santa Claus on a mission to pass the mantle onto the out-of-work host of a failed kid's show. The host, Joe, is torn between his sense of failure and the lure of a potential film career, but if Santa doesn't choose a successor, Christmas will end forever.

Ernest Saves Christmas followed after the success of *Ernest Goes to Camp*, his first flick. Many of the pitchman's signature gags, like chugging from a punch bowl or flipping gravity-defying pancakes, appear in the film and go a long way to prove Varney's comedic sensibility. Running gags and sketch humor elevate the film but no part shines brighter than Douglas Seale as Santa Claus. Best known as the voice of the Sultan in Disney's *Aladdin*, Seale brings charm and repose to Father Christmas. A tiny man, he lacks the girth and the basso voice we usually associate with Papa Noel and is surprisingly gentle, but, despite never appearing in the red suit, you don't doubt for a minute that he's Santa. He is so great that all I could think about while watching the movie was how much I wanted to see him do actual Santa stuff.

My unintended prayer was answered by the discovery of an episode of a TV show called *Amazing Stories*, which ran from 1985 to 1987 and was created by Steven Spielberg.

In the 11th episode, *Santa '85*, Seale portrays another version of Santa who finds himself arrested, this time because a high tech security system catches him. The 24-minute show shares a lot of similarities with *Ernest;* both Santas are arrested, for one, and each has similar "mug shot" scenes. Both see Santa get fingerprinted but with magical results, and both feature a gang of criminals singing "The Twelve Days of Christmas."

If it wasn't for the fact that the *Santa '85* version had a Mrs. Claus you could almost pretend that it's a little story in the life of *Ernest's* Santa. This brings us to one of the more unusual aspects of the *Ernest* Santa: loneliness. Santa doesn't find a potential Mrs. Claus until he has passed the torch on, and even Joe is lonely. The unspoken implication is that being Santa is a solitary life.

Given Santa's connection to selling Coca-Cola and Ernest's to selling literally everything else, you'd think Ernest would have been a better fit for the job than Joe. Either way, *Ernest Saves Christmas* has tremendous heart, in spite of its title character, whose shtick wears thin quickly. I love Ernest, but there are just so many wacky close-ups of him making silly faces that one can take in ninety minutes. Still, Seale as Santa and Noelle Parker as runaway teen Harmony Star, a girl having a crisis of belief, steal the movie.

Santa wants Joe to replace him because Joe loves kids and has dedicated his life to them. Joe's conflicted, however. An offer for a movie career is dangled before him; the only catch is that he'd have to undermine his values and act in a horror movie. Joe's been out of work and feels like a failure in his chosen profession, so it's easy to see why he would be confused; it's a question of integrity.

Integrity is what today's scripture speaks on, despite being about marriage. Integrity means being whole, which is to say, *undivided*. When Paul says unmarried people ought to stay that way it isn't because marriage is bad but because he knows how demanding ministry is. Similarly, there isn't anything wrong with being in a horror movie, it just wasn't right for Joe. Maybe that's why Santa is lonely – the work is all-engrossing. Most of us aren't called to be Santa, but we are called to integrity. We *can* find balance between our duty to the Lord and to others; we *must*, in fact, or we won't be effective with either. I may be paraphrasing a little, but, as it says in Mark 3:25, a divided Santa can't deliver.

JOURNAL QUESTIONS
- Where do you have the most difficulty to find balance?
- Have you ever been tempted to undermine your values for the sake of a job or someone else? How did it turn out?

~ 4 ~
THE YEAR WITHOUT A SANTA CLAUS

"Nobody cares a hoot and a holler for you or Christmas. Oh, by the way, Merry Christmas to you."

Year: 1974
Distributor: Warner Bros. Television
Producer: Joseph Akerman
Directors: Jules Bass, Arthur Rankin Jr.
Writer: William J. Keenan, based on the book by Phyllis McGinley
Runtime: 51 minutes
Rating: Unrated

Scripture Reading: Hebrews 13:17

There are a number of unfortunate stigmas around church. One is against people who only go to church during Christmas and Easter, that their faith is less sincere. Another unfair stigma is that pastors have cushy jobs and only work one day a week. There are certainly pastors who coast, but most are hardworking and can get burnt out, not unlike the Santa in our film today.

While there are large churches with a full and vibrant staff to help carry out the vision of the leadership, in far too many smaller churches the pastor is expected to be a jack-of-all-trades to keep everything running. Even in churches where the pastor doesn't have to also juggle leading a youth group or conducting music or Sunday School classes, most pastors visit the sick, counsel parishioners, and officiate weddings and funerals. Each of those duties requires prep and meetings. This is in addition to the usual preparation for weekly services. Sunday is just the part that others see. A pastor, in his or her way, is like Santa; we only get to see Santa's handiwork on one special morning, but his entire year is spent in preparation.

A lot of pastors share something with the Santa of today's film in particular: burnout. I've often said that there are no part-time pastors, only part-time salaries. A search of the web will direct you to startling statistics regarding clergy burnout. Entire sites are dedicated to providing resources for struggling pastors because such resources seldom exist within the polity of churches. A heart-wrenching amount of pastors lose their marriages over the stress of balancing the needs of their families and the expectations of their congregants, and many report not having any close friends to turn to.[1]

Consider today's film. Santa isn't feeling up to snuff, exacerbated by the belief that the world's children no longer care about him and that he's laboring in vain. This moves him to cancel Christmas and stay in bed for the season. Mrs. Claus, knowing her husband, astutely deduces that what he really needs is a little tender loving care to remind him how much he matters. She sends his two top elves into the world to find some good will, but they mostly find doubters who don't care one way or another, confirming Santa's suspicion.

Part of what makes clergy burnout insidious is that most men and women in career ministry do not treat their positions as *jobs*, but *vocations*. It's their *mission* to serve, so failure (or the perception of failure) weighs heavier on them. Regrettably, a lot of churchgoers don't care what the person behind the pulpit is going through or who they are so long as the job is done and they get what they want out of Sunday. Complicating matters is the notion that pastors are self-sufficient and don't need others because they have God. This assumption is false, inconsiderate, and stands in total contrast with the function of church: *community*. All Christians "have God," but all Christians need support now and then. Why should pastors be different? We might serve different roles, but we are equal members of one Body and

21

must take care of one another. That includes taking care of our pastors and other church leaders.

One of the highlights of today's special is the Snow Miser and Heat Miser, temperamental brothers who rule the weather. Their bickering prevents snow from falling in South Town, a sign that the mayor demands before he'd be willing to help. How many burnt out pastors are made worse by the Heat and Snow Misers of the church, each clutching onto their own territory at the expense of everyone else?

The Year Without a Santa Claus ends with the mayor giving Santa a national holiday and all the world's children coming together to send Santa gifts and to show gratitude for everything he's done for them. This snaps Santa out of his rut and into the sky for the best Christmas ever. As we celebrate Advent, don't forget your church leaders. Not only do they have all of the preparations for themselves and their families that the season brings, but they also have the added work of helping to make your holidays glorious as well. The more you fill their spirits, the more they can give back.

JOURNAL QUESTIONS
- What are some ways you can show your pastor or other spiritual leaders appreciation this holiday season?
- Have you ever experienced burnout in your profession?

~ 5 ~
THE SNOWMAN

"That winter brought the heaviest snow I'd ever seen. The snow fell steadily all through the night. Then, when I woke up, the room was filled with light and silence and I knew then it was to be a magical day."

Year: 1982
Distributor: TVC London
Producer: John Coates
Director: Dianne Jackson
Writer: Based on the book by Raymond Briggs
Runtime: 26 minutes
Rating: U (UK rating meaning Universal for All)

Scripture Reading: 2 Corinthians 4:16-18

Today's film, while growing in popularity in the US, has been a UK Christmas tradition since it debuted back in 1982. Based on the stunning storybook presented wordlessly by artist Raymond Briggs, *The Snowman* tells the story of a little boy named James who makes a snowman that comes to life and takes him on an adventure.

The short was released the day after Christmas on Channel 4 in the UK, which is fitting for two reasons. For one thing, the story of *The Snowman* is more about winter than Christmas. In fact, there are no references to Christmas in the storybook (which, if you don't own, you *must* go out and buy because it is wonderful). While the video features a humble Christmas tree and an appearance from Santa (most likely in an attempt to cement it as a Christmas classic), the book works better without them. Secondly, the story has a sad ending and might be too depressing for kids waiting for Santa's annual visit. Part of why I'm suggesting it so early in this book is to give us plenty of space for happier specials before Christmas arrives.

While the short film climaxes with a sort of "Teddy Bear's Picnic" of snow people at the North Pole, the book is focused on the moments between James and the Snowman. Little things, like sharing a candlelit meal together, go a long way to make the ending more powerful. At the beginning of this book I made it clear that these reflections presume that you've watched the movies in question. No chapter is that more important than this. If you've not seen *The Snowman*, watch it and come back. Otherwise, proceed with caution.

Both the movie and the book end with James racing

to see his new friend the following morning, only to find a melted pile of slush in the dawn sunshine. The movie just stops and the credits roll. It's a startling end for a Christmas program; even to this day I find it haunting. The power of the scene is punctuated by melancholy piano music. For all the changes that were made from the book to the film, this moment is thankfully left intact.

I wasn't introduced to *The Snowman* until I was an adult. When I saw it, I was overwhelmed by the solemnity of the ending and was reminded of something I'd experienced at college not long before. My school had invited a group of Buddhist monks from Tibet. Over the course of several days, the monks constructed a sand mandala, which is a highly intricate "painting" made of various colored sands. A single mandala might contain over 700 individual designs. It was a magnificent display, but I wasn't prepared for the ritual at the end, in which the mandala was destroyed and the sands scattered in our lake. The ceremony represents the Buddhist philosophy of transience, which is to say that the world and everything in it is temporary – like the snowman. Even the sky is an ever-changing canvas, and I'm certain that the most stunning clouds God ever painted in the heavens were seen by no one but Him. Beautiful things aren't always meant to be held onto; sometimes, they exist in their own moment of time and space and our only blessing is just the opportunity to have experienced them while they were here.

Whether it's an expression of creativity like making a snowman, or a beloved pet that passes away, or a candlelit dinner with a charming stranger, eventually dawn comes to claim everything. As it says in our scripture today, the things of the world – even our very bodies – slowly waste away. We can either hang our heads in sorrow like James or we can be like the Snowman and let ourselves get caught up in the wonder of just having had the experience. Every Christmas, truly every *day*, is a new mandala. Each gives us a chance to paint something wonderful and then give it back to the One who offered us the palette.

JOURNAL QUESTIONS

- Have you ever made something which was then destroyed? How did you handle that? Did you make it again, and, if so, was it better, worse, or the same as before?
- How can we take time to appreciate the temporary beauty of the world around us, and how can that connect us more deeply with the Divine?

~ 6 ~
ARTHUR CHRISTMAS

"One child doesn't matter? Which one?"

Year: 2011
Distributor: Columbia Pictures
Producer: Steve Pegram
Director: Sarah Smith
Writers: Peter Baynaham, Sarah Smith
Runtime: 97 minutes
Rating: PG

Scripture Reading: Luke 15:1-7

A refreshing new classic, *Arthur Christmas* is the story of Santa's son Arthur, who is left to work in the mail room because of what a klutz he is. The current Santa, the 20th in the line of succession, is no longer effective, leaving the work to his eldest son, Steve. Treating Christmas like a highly-organized military operation, Steve is dismissive over having missed one child, but Arthur, believing that every child deserves equal effort, sets out with his grandfather and a precocious elf to deliver the child's toy by morning.

Each of the twenty Santas brought their own distinct style to the position. Clearly, Grandsanta represents a more war-weary season of the world. His folksy gumption and flippant regard for the safety of others implies a more rough and tumble cheer-giver than Malcolm (his son, the current Santa). Malcolm is affable but doddering. He has a prim sensibility that calls Nigel Bruce as Dr. Watson in the old Basil Rathbone *Sherlock Holmes* films to mind. Steve, like I said, is militaristic. He's admittedly not good with children but doesn't see why that necessarily makes him a bad Santa. Of all of them, only Arthur typifies Christmas. He is the most sincere in spirit, and his urgency to make sure that not one child is overlooked separates him from the others, who are too concerned with proving themselves or their methods; when they're ready to go to bed, Arthur is ready to *go*.

I'm reminded of the Parable of the Lost Sheep in our reading today. Jesus is chastised by the Pharisees for eating with sinners. He asks them if they had a hundred sheep but one went missing, wouldn't they go and search for it? In the film, both Steve and Malcolm are content to let Gwen go without a gift, focusing instead on all the kids who got their presents, much like the Pharisees were less concerned with individuals than with holding onto their status. Arthur was

28

the good shepherd of the family, understanding that each child deserves the effort. Like the elves asked, if one child doesn't matter, which child is it? To Christ, every single one of us is precious. I would also point out that Jesus suggests in the story that all of us start out on the Nice list but that some of us have wandered. The common interpretation of the parable is that it's about *Christians* who go astray, but Jesus is referring to the *sinners* whom He was with at the time. Everyone is the Lord's (Psalm 24:1), He just doesn't get to *keep* all of us (Mark 16:16).

Before returning to heaven, Jesus gave His apostles the Great Commission, telling them to "make disciples of all nations, baptizing them in the name of the Father and of the Son and of the Holy Spirit, and teaching them to obey everything [He] commanded [them] (Matt. 28:19-20)." Many treat this instruction in a militant, Steve-like way and place enormous emphasis on what they call "soul-winning," which is just an aggressive way of saying "introducing people to Jesus." They count souls like beans in a jar, lifting them with pride. Oh, they'll say it's not about personal glory and add something humble like, "I'm just praising what Christ did through me," but, if they were *really* humble they'd end the sentence with "what Christ did."

We don't win anybody, we simply tell them the good news that they have already been won (Mark 16:15-16), but some Santas cling to that validation like Grandsanta, Steve, and Malcolm fighting over who puts Gwen's bike under the tree. It doesn't matter who makes the introduction, just as it didn't matter who delivered the gift – what matters is that it *happens*. It's important to recognize the key phrase of the verse, *make disciples*. Discipleship is the process of teaching, not the event of staking a claim. An emphasis on numbers can distract us, as it did Steve, and tempt us to overlook the value of each individual. Our Shepherd left the gate open. If someone joins our pen it's because they hear and respond to His voice, not to our effort. It's about Jesus, not us or our methods. Arthur was happy just to be an elf. Likewise, we can be happy being disciples without trying to be Saviors.

JOURNAL QUESTIONS
- Have you ever gotten caught up in disputes over how to do something that really wasn't all that important?
- Have you efforts to "win" someone ever done more harm than good?

~ 7 ~
TWAS THE NIGHT BEFORE CHRISTMAS

"There's more to the world than meets the eye.
When doubt's in your mind give your
heart a try."

Year: 1974
Distributor: Film Roman, United Media Paws, Inc.
Producer: Phil Roman
Directors: Jules Bass, Arthur Rankin Jr.
Writer: Jerome Coopersmith, based on the poem by Clement
Clarke Moore
Runtime: 25 minutes
Rating: TV-G

Scripture Reading: 2 Chronicles 7:12-18

The more you watch Christmas specials, the more
you begin to notice that so many of them focus on a crisis
of belief. Skepticism over Santa is a central theme in today's
entry as well. *Twas the Night Before Christmas* expands on
Clement Moore's poem with the added drama of a village in
peril over the fear that Santa might not come. I use the word

peril because to hear the townspeople go on about it, you'd think they were more worried about of the retribution of an angry god than just not getting free toys one year.

In a world where humans and mice live in a peaceful harmony, the son of a clock-worker mouse writes a scathing open letter to Santa, denouncing any belief in him and his flying reindeer. He signs the letter "all of us," which leads to Santa dismissing the entire village and sending their letters back unopened. The town scrambles over what to do to gain Santa's favor again. The human clock maker that the mouse works with suggests building a Babel-like clock tower which, at midnight, would play a song that will hopefully appease Santa as he zooms by. It goes "kerplowie" when the skeptical mouse child who wrote the letter, Albert, goes into the clock tower and accidentally breaks it. So Albert, understanding that "sometimes a miracle needs a hand," sets out to fix the clock tower, not sure of what he believes but conceding he still has a lot to learn. He fixes the clock just in time! Santa hears the song and brings Christmas cheer to the town, and Albert learns a valuable lesson about seeing things with one's heart rather than with one's head.

'Twas the Night Before Christmas has a lot of charm, but I've always had some problems with it. Santa supposedly

32

knows when you are awake or asleep. He has lists that divide the world's children into groups of Naughty and Nice. He knows who doesn't believe in him, because those kids don't get presents. How, then, would an op-ed signed "all of us" trick him into thinking it actually represented everybody? If Santa is so commonly accepted that people literally pace the halls on Christmas Eve out of the fear that he might pass them by, why does Albert even question his existence? Lastly, and probably most importantly, *so what if he doesn't come?*

If there is one message that almost every Christmas special has drilled into our heads it's that Christmas is more than presents. Imagine an alternate version of the special where instead of fixing the clock, the townspeople gather around it and sing like the Whos from *The Grinch*, realizing they don't need gifts to celebrate. Having learned a lesson about what's actually important, the town is *then* visited by Santa. Sure, it would be a flagrant ripoff of Dr. Seuss, but it would be a nicer story and would offer a less terrible picture of Santa, who everyone seems to cower in fear of like he might smite them.

This image of Santa as a fickle god who rewards the faithful but punishes entire cities for the disbelief of a few is sadly not too hard a pill to swallow when one considers how people throughout history, and today, picture God. Not to say that there's no reason for that, of course. Scripture is filled with indictments against the entirety of Israel because of its citizens who turned to false gods. Today's scripture is a go-to for those who are dispirited by culture and fear we are in the end times because of it, but they miss the point; God withheld blessings from the land when *His children* sinned, not *unbelievers*. He already knows *they* don't believe, but do *you* believe enough to trust Him when things look hopeless?

How do you see God? Is He like Santa in our special today, withholding blessings for wrongs that aren't our fault? The fear of the Lord is the beginning of wisdom (Proverbs 9:10), but it isn't the end. Just like falling is the beginning of walking, spiritual maturity carries us beyond Fear and into His Peace (Philippians 4:7). Fear doesn't come from God (2 Timothy 1:7), but the first steps towards Him can be scary, so we should do everything we can to help the Alberts of the world and lend their miracle a hand.

JOURNAL QUESTIONS
- What has been the scariest step in your spiritual journey?
- How can we "lend a hand" to miracles?

~ 8 ~
THE BISHOP'S WIFE

"Sometimes angels rush in where fools fear to tread."

Year: 1947
Distributor: RKO Radio Pictures
Producer: Samuel Goldwyn
Director: Henry Koster
Writers: Robert E. Sherwood, Leonardo Bercovici
Runtime: 109 minutes
Rating: Not Rated

Scripture Reading: James 2:1-7

Cary Grant, David Niven, and Loretta Young star in this tender exploration of the pitfalls of career ministry. Bishop Henry Broughman struggles to finance a cathedral, spending most of his time placating demanding backers. His marriage to his wife, Julia, languishes as a result. A desperate prayer invites a charismatic angel named Dudley who turns Henry's life upside-down; Dudley convinces the cathedral's donor to give her money to the needy and he inadvertently woos the bishop's wife, growing too attached himself.

Dudley's presence alienates Henry from Julia further, prompting Henry to finally stand up and fight for her and his family. Dudley indicates that this was his goal all along, making Henry jealous enough to see that his priorities have been skewed; what the bishop needed was to cherish what he had, not hustle for more. We meet several characters over the course of the movie, friends whom Henry has forgotten while drowning in his work. The film ends with Henry and Julia's marriage restored; Dudley exits and takes all memory of his visit with him but leaves behind a grumpy cab driver with a warmed heart and a doubting old professor with fresh faith and a sense of purpose.

Grant's boundless energy carries the film. He shifts effortlessly from bouncy charmer to serious messenger. The movie does an exceptional job of portraying the unspoken stresses of career ministry and gently reminds us that the best of us can lose focus. For a movie about church life, *The Bishop's Wife* is surprisingly disenfranchised by it. When he looks over the cathedral designs, Dudley comments that its large roof could provide so many little ones, a critique of excessive church spending. Julia muses over the tiny parish where Henry served before he become a bishop, emphasizing the value of relationships over success. Henry's lost his way, motivated by ambition rather than a heart for service. He's smug, having no trouble ordering servants around. Compare his behavior with Jesus, who said that He came to serve others, not be served (Mark 10:45). Ephesians 5:25 instructs husbands to love their wives the way Jesus loved the church; Jesus showed his love though self-sacrifice. Henry spends more time dealing with Mrs. Hamilton, the wealthy donor who's funding the cathedral and who got him the position of bishop, than with Julia. Seeing him chase Mrs. Hamilton while Dudley spends his time with the everyday folk Henry has left behind calls James 2:1-5 to mind, which warns us to not show partiality to the rich and to remember that Jesus' heart is with the poor in spirit.

Ironically, this film about conflicting objectives and over-budget monoliths mirrored its production. The movie was originally directed by William A. Seiter, but he was fired by producer Samuel Goldwyn, who replaced him with Henry Koster when he didn't like the footage he was seeing. When filming began, Cary Grant played Henry and Dudley was played by David Niven. It's hard to picture the milquetoast Niven as the ebullient Dudley. Koster felt the same way and wanted them to switch, but Grant didn't wish to because he desired the title billing. Petty disputes broke out amongst the stars over not feeling like they were being shot properly, and the finished film cost an additional $1 million to complete, which would be about $11 million today. Did any of them *read* the script? Did the words about not letting a "me first" attitude get in the way of doing the right thing penetrate their hearts while they were speaking them?

The movie ends with Henry giving a Christmas Eve sermon secretly written by Dudley. He asks us not to forget to fill Christ's stocking as we fill everyone else's. He suggests that Jesus would ask for loving-kindness, warm hearts, and a stretched out hand of tolerance; "all the shining gifts that make peace on earth." We might never have peace on earth, but we can do our part by living peaceably (Romans 8:12) and by treasuring what we have. We can't stretch out a hand of tolerance while reaching for our own self-interests, and loving-kindness lives in the present, which also happens to be where the real work of ministry resides too.

JOURNAL QUESTIONS
- Do you struggle to show partiality?
- How can we find contentment living in the present?

~ 9 ~
THE TOWN SANTA FORGOT

"Yes, every few Christmases Santa must choose a new boy or girl for his Christmas Eve cruise to help him deliver the toys down the floo. To help drive the reindeer. Will it be you?"

Year: 1993
Distributor: Hanna-Barbera Productions
Producers: David Kirchner, Davis Doi
Director: Robert Alvarez
Writer: Glenn Leopold, from the poem by Charmaine Severson
Runtime: 23 minutes
Rating: Not Rated

Scripture Reading: Ephesians 6:1-4

The Town Santa Forgot is the story of Jeremy Creek, an obnoxious child who sends Santa a list a half mile long. Santa thinks it must be for a town rather than a single child and actually finds a village called Jeremy Creek that he never visited. Bringing them the toys Jeremy asked for not only gives those kids hope but also softens Jeremy's heart, earning him a spot in the sleigh as Santa's assistant.

Jeremy Creek reminds me of another red-haired boy I once knew when I was early in my youth ministry career. My "Jeremy" was also a bit of a trouble maker but wasn't quite so greedy. He was rambunctious, though, and stubborn. At the time, I coordinated a children's church program for kids Kindergarten through 5th Grade, and I needed help. I also believed that the best way to make someone responsible was by giving them responsibility, so, not unlike the Santa in today's special, I asked Jeremy to assist me and he jumped at the chance. He himself was only in 6th Grade, making him just a year older than the oldest students in my class, but he was great with the kids. Naturally, I never gave him anything too big to do, with my adult volunteers handling most of the "heavy lifting," but just thinking he was my right hand motivated him to step up.

We had only one impasse, at Rock the Universe, an annual concert event held at Universal Studios, Orlando. We had a rule that while high schoolers could be on their own in groups of three or more, middle schoolers needed to be with an adult. Jeremy broke away from our group and went off on his own, leaving me to wander the deserted streets of Universal Studios until 2 a.m. searching for him. It was a Saturday night, and, thanks to Jeremy, we wouldn't get back to our church until after 4 a.m.. I didn't show my anger, but I made it clear that I was disappointed. I told Jeremy that he wouldn't be helping me the next morning, and that was enough to keep him from acting up again. Not surprisingly, he had a troubled home life, and, in some ways, he treated me like a second father. Years later, after I was long gone from his church, I can remember late nights when he'd call me in tears over hardships that he was dealing with.

Today's reading tells children to obey their parents but reminds parents not to exasperate them. I chuckle when I read it, because I always imagined it as a sort of ironic threat. "Hey, you wanna live a long life? Then knock it off!" When I saw Jeremy in the beginning of the show, pounding his fists and screaming, all I could think of was the spanking I'd have gotten if it was me. Whether we should spank our kids or not is a debate for another time, but our modern saying to "spare the rod and spoil the child" misunderstands scripture, implying that we should go light on discipline and indulge our kids. The expression means the opposite: *if* you spare then rod, *then* you spoil the child. *Spoil* doesn't mean *indulge;* it means *ruin.*

Too often, we confuse *discipline* with *punishment.* Punishing someone is about making ourselves feel better by venting our anger; discipline is about the well-being of the other person and means to *train*. Consider Jeremy's parents in the special. Rather than correcting his behavior, they cave to his every whim and give him whatever he wants. When they reach their breaking point, they yell at him and refuse to buy him more toys, but they don't replace that with any sort of good behavior. They treated *stuff* as a surrogate for *time*, so when the "stuff" was gone he was left with nothing. Even if it was by accident, Santa giving Jeremy's toys away did something that his parents' neglect couldn't: taught him a lesson, giving him the opportunity to grow.

Obviously, a lot of families struggle over challenging work schedules or having only one parent to juggle all of the responsibilities. Time management is difficult but essential. During this season of giving, regardless of what lovely things we buy one another, may we always be mindful of how we might give the most priceless and irreplaceable gift; time.

JOURNAL QUESTIONS
- What are the gifts you've most appreciated giving? Getting?
- What are practical ways to help make time for loved ones?

~ 10 ~
SANTA CLAUS: THE MOVIE

"If you give extra kisses, you get bigger hugs."

Year: 1985
Distributor: TriStar Pictures
Producers: Pierre Spengler, Ilya Salkind
Director: Jeannot Szwarc
Writer: David Newman
Runtime: 107 minutes
Rating: PG

Scripture Reading: Matthew 25:1-13

Today's film is polarizing. From the director of such "hits" as *Jaws 2* and *Supergirl*, *Santa Claus: The Movie* is a bizarre attempt to interpret Santa's lore with the sensibility of *Superman: The Movie*.[1] Both films even end with a man flying past the earth and looking at the camera. Claus is a toy maker from Scandinavia who nearly freezes to death with his wife on Christmas Eve while delivering gifts. They are rescued by the vendegum, beings who prefer to be called elves and live in an invisible ice world. A fortress of solitude, you might say. They've been preparing for Claus for a long

43

time; a prophecy said a toy maker would come who loved children and would give their gifts to the world. Becoming Santa, Claus montages through the centuries, delivering gifts and building his legend. Santa is moved by a homeless boy named Joe when he arrives in 80's New York. Joe is smitten with a girl named Cornelia who leaves him food. Her step-uncle, B.Z., is an evil CEO who runs a toy company and was modeled after Gene Hackman in *Superman*.

An uppity elf named Patch tries to prove himself as Santa's assistant by building an assembly-line-style machine to create the toys for the year, but it fails and all the gifts break, humiliating Santa. Patch steps down, and the job goes to an elf named Puffy who isn't as *productive* as Patch but strives for excellence. Hoping to regain Santa's favor, Patch leaves and joins B.Z., creating lollipops that make kids float, but all B.Z. sees is a potential fortune, so he convinces Patch to make a more potent formula that he can sell as candy canes which will make children fly.

Joe is caught eavesdropping with Cornelia, and he is taken away, but Cornelia learns that the candy canes explode with heat, so she sends Santa a letter, begging for help. Joe is discovered by Patch, who decides to take him and the candy canes to the North Pole, not knowing that they will explode.

The finale is a race against time as Santa tries to catch Patch and Joe before Patch's magic flying car blows up.

The film earned just $23 million of its $50 million budget back and garnered mostly negative reviews. Still, it's gained a cult following and is one of my favorite Christmas movies. So far as I was concerned, David Huddleston was the real Santa, and I believed in the movie because of the weight it gave everything. With the exception of B.Z., who gobbles up scenery like magic candy canes, everyone takes it seriously. The scene when the Ancient Elf, played by Burgess Meredith, anoints Santa has tremendous power. Scenes like when Patch resigns or when Santa grieves to his wife about it are intensely dramatic; the movie doesn't have a lot of *story*, but it has a whole lot of *heart*.

There's a tender moment early in the film in the Toy Tunnel, an endless warehouse of the toys that the elves made anticipating Santa's arrival. They toiled for centuries because they believed so strongly in the prophecy that Santa would come. I'm reminded of the parable about ten virgins who were told to wait and greet a groom with lanterns. Five wise ones stood watch and had lanterns ready, but the other five were unwise; they not only didn't fill their lanterns with oil but also fell asleep. When the groom arrived, it was too late

45

and they were left out of the wedding. The parable is about Jesus' return. We don't know when He will come back, so we should be shrewd with our time. The elves were like the wise virgins, working with the confidence that their faith would be rewarded.

I got to be an elf once, on my school's float for a Christmas parade when I was in fifth grade. My job was to sit at the front, which was Santa's toy shop, and hammer at toys. I kept forgetting to, though, because, as a fifth grader, I felt like a star and kept waving at the crowd instead. As I think of the elves, working in hope that Santa would come, I wonder how often I'm like the unwise virgins in the parable. We preach that Jesus will come back, but do we live like it? Do we roll up our sleeves and hammer away or do we smile and wave? Then again, some believers are like Patch, way too zealous and doing more harm than good. We find balance being like Puffy, knowing the Christmas Eve deadline will come but working in steady excellence until it does.

JOURNAL QUESTIONS
- How can a competitive spirit get in the way of Christmas?
- How can we live in the present and be mindful of the fact we have an unknown spiritual "deadline?"

~ 11 ~
THE SMURFS CHRISTMAS SPECIAL

"Maybe anything *can* happen. Even miracles."

Year: 1982
Distributor: NBC
Producer: Gerard Baldwin
Director: Gerard Baldwin
Writers: Len Janson and Chuck Menville, from a story by Garard Baldwin, Peyo, and Yvan Delporte
Runtime: 24 minutes
Rating: Not Rated

Scripture Reading: Luke 6:43-45

Remember that one time the Smurfs battled Satan on Christmas Eve? True, the 1982 *Smurfs Christmas Special* never comes out and directly *calls* "the Stranger" Satan, but the signs are there. From his pointy black beard, his allusion that goodness comes his way only by betrayal, and the fact that the supernatural "home" he was taking his victims to was a fiery place of terror, it's pretty clear. Even Papa Smurf

47

recognizes something uniquely evil about him. The Stranger bargains with Gargamel, giving him the means to find and destroy the Smurfs' village in exchange for kidnapping the two children of a local nobleman. It may seem out of place to make the devil the villain of a Christmas special, but the bible does it too.

In Revelation 12, we see the story of Christmas from a different perspective. It illustrates a vision of a woman in labor and a dragon chomping for her newborn. That child, of course, is Jesus, and the dragon is Satan. The passage is understood to be a reference to the infanticide ordered by Herod, a part of Christmas that we seldom discuss. Perhaps our nativities should include a dragon to remind us of what was defeated in that humble stable.

Towards the end of the special, the Stranger has the children tied up and is holding Gargamel prisoner in a ring of fire, part of a ceremony to transport them, presumably, to hell. Smurfette, overwhelmed by the apparent hopelessness of the scene, asks Papa Smurf what they could do against such evil power. Papa Smurf reminds her that the power of love is greater, and so the Smurfs band together and sing an old holiday carol to vanquish the demon. The children, and even Gargamel, add their voices from within the ring of fire, and the Stranger fades away. Our dog would always howl at that part when I was a child. I like to think he trying to sing along and wasn't, you know, being exorcised.

It's a peculiar way of defeating an enemy, no less the devil himself, but Christians ought to be familiar with the strategy if they've read Joshua 6. At the wall of Jericho, God instructs Joshua that, instead of trying to break through and take the city by force, he and his army are to circle the wall once a day for six days and then, on the seventh, all join together in blowing horns around it. The wall comes down when they blow their horns, and they ambush the city. Why does this work? Was it something about the harmonics of the horns or the wall being shaken by the sound waves? No. It had nothing to do with the horns; it had to do with the power at work in the hearts of those who trumpeted them.

We're just vessels; we can hold bitterness and ugliness or we can open ourselves up to Love's light, a power so great we can hardly contain it. It's the difference between blowing smoke into a bottle versus filling it with water. The bottle is the same, but the density of that clean, nourishing water is so much greater than the fog which clouds our minds when we labor in hate. Even when we feel as small as a Smurf, just three apples tall, we can extinguish the flames of the dragon because we can hold more of God's living water in our spirit than the dragon has room for smoke in his throat.

The special ends with the Stranger defeated and the children returned to their uncle, but the Smurf village is in ruins. In one last connection to the biblical story of Jericho, Harmony Smurf asks to play his trumpet solo for his fellow 99 Smurfs in the hopes of warming their hearts on the cold, sad Christmas Eve night. Inexplicably, the power of his solo has a magic of its very own, and the village is restored! Our scripture today echoes the words of the Smurfs' song, saying good things come from the good stored within us. "Badness cannot start if there's is goodness in your heart," because there won't be room for it. It's up to you to choose what to fill yourself with.

JOURNAL QUESTIONS

- Have you had "Jericho" moments when God directed you to do something that made no sense but produced results?
- What are some ways we can "store up" good in our hearts?

~ 12 ~
OLIVE, THE OTHER REINDEER

"Unorthodox style, but whatever works."

Year: 1999
Distributor: 20th Television
Producers: John A. Davis, Matt Groening
Director: Steve Moore
Writer: Steve Young, based on the book by J. Otto Siebold and Vivian Walsh
Runtime: 45 minutes
Rating: Not Rated

Scripture Reading: 1 Corinthians 12:4-11

I had never heard of *Olive, the Other Reindeer* until a friend recommended it to me. Doing no research prior to viewing, I was encouraged by a surprising credit: Executive Producer Matt Groening, famous for creating *Futurama* and *The Simpsons.* I settled in, unsure of what to expect.

Olive is a dog whose master constantly berates her for not being dog-like enough. She's so unlike a dog that she has a pet flea! The constant pressure of her master leads her to believe that she isn't really a dog at all, at least not *inside.*

Listening to the radio, she learns that Santa is canceling his flight because one of his reindeer is sick. Her pet flea, Fido, mishears Santa's call for "all of the other reindeer" to help and thinks he said "Olive, the other reindeer." Confirming her suspicion that she isn't meant to be a dog, Olive sets out for the North Pole believing that she's a reindeer.

Olive makes friends with a penguin who has escaped from the zoo and sells fake watches in alleys, and makes an enemy in a lunatic Postman who's delighted that Christmas is canceled because of the extra work that the season puts on his shoulders. He tries to stop her from reaching the North Pole and has been sending mean letters to Santa pretending to be children in the hopes of making Claus quit.

Olive is able to convince Santa that he is still loved and that the villainous Postman is behind everything. She even convinces him that she's a reindeer and to let her join the sleigh team (despite not being able to fly). The Postman steals Santa's bag in one last attempt at stopping Christmas, but Olive, being a dog, tracks him down with her nose. She returns as a hero, and Tim, her owner, finally appreciates her for the dog that she is rather than the dog that he thinks she should be. More importantly, Olive is finally content to be a dog because she's allowed to be herself.

In our scripture today, Paul explains how the Spirit gives us different gifts for different kinds of ministry. Just as "Olive" wasn't a reindeer, "all of" us aren't pastors, nor are "all of" us healers or teachers, but "all of" us have a part to play, even if we don't always know what it is. Complicating matters are the well-intended (and not-so-well-intended) folks who are happy to tell us. In much the same way that Olive's master, Tim, tries training her to be the dog he thinks she should be, we get "trained" by people who think they know best and can grow as frustrated as Olive trying to reconcile their expectations with who we believe we're meant to be.

Because of my talents, I let myself become convinced that I should be a pastor. In my denomination, that process is strenuous. It requires a psychological evaluation (because, honestly, who in their right mind wants to be a pastor?), as well as a mentor group with other candidates. Eventually, we meet with District representatives who attempt to determine whether we have a legitimate calling on our hearts or not.

When I met with them, they thought I was educated and well-spoken but didn't detect that *I* believed I was called. They were right; deep down, I had rationalized that I *could be* a pastor, but I didn't really believe that I *should be*. I had qualities that would make me effective, but after two years of the process I surrendered to what I already knew and bowed out to pursue what I believe is a better fit for me, and you're reading one of the results of that choice.

In my defense, no one else from my mentor group became a pastor either. That's what the process is designed for – helping us discern whether we are called be a pastor (a specific role) or called to be in ministry (which applies to us all). Not everyone is a reindeer, but everyone has a place in Santa's team regardless of the expectations of others. How many languish in jobs that they hate just because someone they trusted told them that's what they were meant for? It's hard work to find your "calling," and it takes courage to live authentically. Frederick Buechner wrote that vocation is "the place where your deep gladness and the world's deep hunger meet."[1] What's your calling? I can't say. *I'm not supposed to.* That discovery is for you, but 'all of' us are on that journey together.

JOURNAL QUESTIONS
- Do you believe that you've identified a calling in your life?
- Have you ever tried to do something that you believed you should do but knew wasn't right for you?

~ 13 ~
A GARFIELD CHRISTMAS SPECIAL

"All right, you guys, just permit me one sentimental moment here, will you? I have something to say. Christmas: it's not the giving, it's not the getting, it's the loving. There, I said it. Now get outta here. "

Year: 1987
Distributor: Film Roman, United Media Paws, Inc.
Producer: Phil Roman
Directors: Phil Roman, George Singer
Writer: Jim Davis
Runtime: 30 minutes
Rating: TV-G

Scripture Reading: Hebrews 13:5

Having had success two years prior with *Garfield's Halloween Adventure, A Garfield Christmas Special* adds to the Arbuckle family by introducing us to Jon's homey mom, no-nonsense dad, irascible brother, and firebrand grandma. Grandma, voiced by Pat Carroll, keeps to herself during the bustle of the holidays, reminiscing with Garfield about her late husband and feeling disconnected.

Most people know Pat Carroll as the voice of Ursula in Disney's *The Little Mermaid*, the role that likely got her invited to Spooky Empire's May-Hem convention in 2014. It featured an eclectic assortment of performers, such as actors from horror films like *Halloween* and *A Nightmare on Elm Street*, musical guests like Doyle from The Misfits and Lita Ford, and the cast of *Once Upon a Time*. Even Godzilla was there. The person I most wanted to meet was Pat.

My friend Justin and I were near the end of the line as the final day of the convention drew to a close. They were packing up the various collectibles and head shots that she had available to autograph when her representative informed us that they were selling the poster from *The Little Mermaid* which hung over her booth. I was able to claim it, but not before a wonderful talk with the sea witch herself.

We never discussed Ursula, though; we talked about *Garfield* and how my family watches it every season (along with the Thanksgiving special, which she also appears in). I told her how we always debate over whether Grandma is the father's mother or the mother's mother. We have compelling arguments for either, but I maintain that she's the mother's mom and is secretly spiteful of her daughter. Pat laughed in her unmistakable, throaty cackle and told me that Jim Davis never did say whose mother she was. I have met a number of truly wonderful actors at conventions over the years, but her warmth was infectious. She seemed to be genuinely touched by our conversation, telling me that in all of her convention experiences I was the first person to ever talk about *Garfield*. Her children and grandkids helped run the booth, and even after my friend and I moved aside for other attendees they continued to talk with us and make us feel like part of their family. Justin and I left glowing, both of us wishing we had a grandma like Grandma.

The special opens with Garfield dreaming that Jon gave him a machine that looks like Santa's lap and can give you anything you can imagine. Within seconds, a mountain of treasure erupts from Santa's bag. If you look closely, you will notice that they recycled several sequences over and over (to cut production costs). By the end of the scene, Garfield has dozens of toasters, planes, bowling balls, and turkeys. This budgetary decision is an unintended commentary that if Christmas is nothing but stuff, after a while it all becomes a meaningless blur.

Grandma largely goes ignored by the family, caught up in their festivities. Garfield presents her with the best gift of the day - a stack of love letters written to her by her late husband. "Stuff" is great, but nothing compares with tender memories of cherished loved ones. Our passage warns not to get absorbed with material wealth, referencing Deuteronomy 31:6, in which God promises never to forsake us. It seems an odd connection; what does wealth have to do with God not forsaking us? It's because an obsession with money reveals a fear over *security*. Wealth gives us the *feeling* of security but can't accomplish the task of truly *making* us secure anymore than it can provide lasting joy; rather, joy and security come from *connection*. There's nothing wrong with having things, of course – the question is does God have *you?*

One of my favorite "things," and one which I feel no shame in displaying, is a *Little Mermaid* poster that wishes me "Oceans of love" from Pat Carroll. Meeting her and being welcomed by her family made me feel, for a moment, like I was part of the animated family I've watched countless times. It was a little Christmas in May and is one of my favorite holiday memories.

JOURNAL QUESTIONS
- What would wish for if you had Garfield's dream machine?
- When do you feel the most secure? How can you cultivate that feeling in all the areas of your life?

~ 14 ~
JACK FROST

"The happiness of being me is not what it's cracked up to be. It's lonely being one of a kind."

Year: 1979
Distributor: Lorimar Telepictures/Warner Bros. Television
Producers: Jules Bass, Arthur Rankin Jr.
Directors: Jules Bass, Arthur Rankin Jr.
Writer: Romeo Muller
Runtime: 48 minutes
Rating: Not Rated

Scripture Reading: Matthew 13:45-46

This lesser known Rankin/Bass special is a story of unrequited love. Jack Frost, the spirit of winter, falls in love with Elisa, a maiden who adores the season. Jack confuses her sentimentality for genuine affection, which leads him to question his happiness as a spirit. Incapable of interacting with the human world, he becomes aware of a loneliness he never felt before and sets out to become a mortal human so that he can win her hand.

Jack strikes a bargain with Father Winter, who allows him to have a "winter of humanity" with a promise that he can become mortal forever if, by the first of spring, Jack can secure "a house to shelter him, a horse to bear him, a bag of gold to sustain him, and a wife to make it worth the while." Jack is clumsy as a mortal and even slips on ice. Elisa is there to help, but this is where Jack makes his first mistake. Before his transformation, Jack saved Elisa's life from an ice drift heading towards a waterfall. He could reveal himself as Jack Frost, who saved her life, but doesn't. He pretends to be a tailor named Jack Snip, instead. His second mistake is not paying attention. Upon meeting, Elisa dismisses Jack, saying that he isn't the gold knight that she's been waiting for; she wasn't interested in Jack, but, like many young men blinded by attraction, he doesn't see that he never stood a chance.

The village is oppressed by a Cossack tyrant named Kubla Kraus who is so unlikable that he's been abandoned by all of his kin, leaving him alone in his castle with only a clockwork army and a hand puppet to keep him company. Kubla kidnaps Elisa, planning to force her into marriage, but Jack and his friends mount a rescue, joined by an actual knight in golden armor who has come home for Christmas. Enraged at having Elisa snatched from him, Kubla declares war on the village, vowing to destroy it with his clockwork army. Jack surrenders his mortality so that he can keep the castle snowbound using his powers. He saves the village, but this gives Elisa and the knight time to fall in love.

Within an hour of spring, Jack has claimed his gold, house, and horse by defeating Kubla, so Father Winter lets him be a human a little bit longer to marry Elisa. Sadly, it's too late, and he arrives just in time for Elisa and the Knight to be wed. The clock chimes noon on the first day of spring and Jack fades back into the realm of the ethereal as his one, true love marries another man. He blows a whisper of frost across Elisa's bouquet, which she recognizes as a kiss from an old friend, and he flies back into the sky. The show ends with a joyful homecoming for Jack in the clouds to distract us from the sad ending. Jack's sudden, chipper attitude never sat well with me and always seemed like a cop-out.

Love is paradoxical. It drives us to give of ourselves and sacrifice for another while hoping to have that person for our own. Love is both the most selfless *and* selfish thing we can experience. As I watch this film, I wonder what it was like for Jesus, looking down from heaven and longing to be with us. What conversations did He and the Father have in preparation, knowing that winning His one, true love would cost Him everything? Jesus could have come demanding the world's devotion, but that wouldn't be love. Jack erroneously believed that he could *earn* Elisa's love by obtaining a house, gold, and a horse, but that isn't how love works. The hardest lesson about love that we'll ever learn is that no amount of loving someone will ever make them love us back.

In today's passage, Jesus compares the Church to a man who finds a pearl and spends everything he has so that he could buy the field where he found it. The story is often interpreted that Jesus is the pearl and we should give up everything for Him, but it means the opposite; *we are that pearl.* *Jesus* paid everything for *us*, just like Jack was willing to give up immortality for Elisa. In much the same way as Jack's overtures of love didn't promise success, Jesus' success depends on us; He may have bought the field, but it is our choice to either offer Christ the pearl of our heart or make Him watch His true love choose whatever gold knight we chase after, instead.

JOURNAL QUESTIONS
- Have you ever loved someone who didn't love you back? If so, what happened? Were you ultimately grateful?
- How can knowing you're the pearl help your self worth?

~ 15 ~
FROSTY'S WINTER WONDERLAND

"I told them I'd be back again someday, but when will someday come?"

Year: 1976
Distributor: Warner Bros. Home Media
Producers: Jules Bass, Arther Rankin Jr.
Directors: Jules Bass, Arthur Rankin Jr.
Writer: Romeo Muller
Runtime: 25 minutes
Rating: Not Rated

Scripture Reading: Genesis 2:4-25

Allow me to indulge in a bit of fan speculation. As someone who saw *Jack Frost* before seeing today's entry, it's always griped me that the once noble Jack was the villain. I like to think that the Rankin/Bass specials exist in their own shared universe, with all of the specials interconnected. Why, then, is he so different? They wear the same costume. They're physically similar, except that the cartoon Jack is plumper

63

and older. They both whistle for their winter powers. Maybe they *are* the same Jack, but changed. I discussed in the prior entry how frustrated I have always been with how perky and happy Jack appears at the end, having lost all hope of being with his true love, but as I reflect on today's special I see that ending in a different light. Remember what Father Winter said about Jack's time on earth – it was merely a "winter of humanity." Perhaps he didn't only lose his one, true love as a result of his wager to find happiness as a mortal but any remaining humanity as well. What would happen to a cold, lonely being like Jack if he was robbed of any humanity? He would likely dig into himself, becoming arrogant, entitled, and bitter, not unlike how we see him in today's film. And what was it that snapped Jack out of his rut and helped him rediscover his humanity? The very thing that he himself was denied – a wedding.

Unlike Jack, Frosty is able to interact with humans and enjoy the companionship of others. Frosty even found a bride, and he didn't have to grovel to Father Winter to get one. Frosty bumbles his way into it everything Jack wanted. Jack's love was different, though. He only believed Elisa was in love with him because of how she stroked his ego. This is a pretty consistent theme with Jack. At his center, he doesn't want to be *loved* so much as he wants to be *adored*. Perhaps this is why Crystal's flattery and request for him to be Best Man at her and Frosty's wedding was effective.

Jack didn't really need a wife because he was in love with himself. Frosty, on the other hand, felt the loneliness of being out in the cold after his friends went home. The story of Frosty and Crystal is a touching way of imaging what it might have been like for Adam; night would fall over Eden, but while the animals each curled up with their others he was alone. Adam felt a need that he could likely not explain. He'd never seen a woman before, just as Frosty had no idea what a wife was, but once Crystal arrived Frosty no longer needed a magic hat to keep him going: her love was enough. There are a lot of Frostys out there longing for their Crystal and a lot of Crystals out there hoping some Frosty is smart enough to offer her his bouquet. Our happiness shouldn't depend on being in a relationship, of course, but the story of Frosty and Crystal rings true for many of us. One person it rings true for, someone we seldom think about waiting for his Bride, is Jesus.

Jesus and Frosty are a lot alike. Christmas *is* a happy birthday for Frosty, after all. Both are pure, best understood through the lens of child-like innocence, and died but were resurrected. Also, both left but promised to come back. The bible refers to the Church as the Bride of Christ, a metaphor that articulates the love and yearning Jesus feels while He waits and wonders when He will be able to return. Like any lovelorn man who anticipates meeting the girl of his dreams, Jesus doesn't know when that day will come (Mark 13:32-33).

Every day feels like winter if you are lonely enough. The cold of such a winter can penetrate the heart, like it did Jack Frost, if we're not careful. Some of us thought we found our Crystal or Frosty, only to end up in a union more bitter than the harshest blizzard. Others continue to wait for love to arrive at all. In all our longings, we have a friend in Jesus; He knows better than any of us what it is to wait, and can warm the coldest hearts throughout all the seasons of life.

JOURNAL QUESTIONS
- How can remembering that Christ waits for his Church be a comfort in lonely, difficult times?
- What do you think makes for the perfect spouse? What has informed your standards for good relationships?

~ 16 ~
FRED CLAUS

"There's no naughty kids, Nick. They're all good kids. But some of them are scared, and some of them don't feel listened to. Some of them had some pretty tough breaks, too, but every kid deserves a present on Christmas."

Year: 2007
Distributor: Warner Bros. Pictures
Producers: Joel Silver, David Dobkin, Paul Hitchcock, and Jessie Nelson
Director: David Dobkin
Writer: Dan Fogelman
Runtime: 116 minutes
Rating: PG

Scripture Reading: Luke 15:11-32

An underrated treat with an amazing cast including Kathy Bates, Kevin Spacey, and Paul Giamatti as a stressed, over-worked Santa, *Fred Claus* is the story of Santa's older, ne'er-do-well brother. Fred wants to take advantage of his famous brother but saves the day when a devious efficiency expert threatens to cancel Christmas forever.

I don't know why the film performed poorly, barely making back its $100 million budget. Aside from some odd creative choices, like cartoon sound effects where they don't belong, *Fred Claus* is a humorous, heart-felt interpretation of Santa which depicts a side of him that we seldom get to see – tired and afraid. Giamatti has spent centuries being a people-pleaser and it's taking its toll. Kevin Spacey shines as Cylde, the slimy efficiency expert looking to crack down on Santa and end Christmas. Spacey portrayed Lex Luthor in *Superman Returns* the year prior, so the exchange between Giamatti and Spacey about how all Clyde wanted was to be Superman growing up was especially enjoyable for a comic book nerd like me. It's also the crux of the film's theme: *be careful how you judge.*

This story about the disconnect between two brothers reminds me of another story about brothers. Luke 15 offers the parable of a son who lost his way. Demanding his share of his father's estate, he sets out and blows it on wild living. Starving, he hires himself out as a servant and is so hungry that the slop he was feeding pigs looked good. Coming to his senses, he resolves to go to his father and beg him to hire him like a servant, but, as his father sees him draw near he runs out and embraces him and calls for a celebration. The older brother is spiteful. "Look," he says to his father. "All these years I've been slaving for you and never disobeyed your orders. Yet you never gave me even a young goat so I could celebrate with my friends. But when this son of yours who has squandered your property with prostitutes comes home, you kill the fattened calf for him!" The father tries to help him understand that the important thing was that his brother was home again, but scripture doesn't say if he was successful.

The parable isn't exactly like Fred's story. There is no mediating father figure, and Nick always hoped his brother would come around. Still, as I watch the movie and consider its themes about being too quick to brush off someone as "naughty," I can't help but think of the bitter brother who stayed. He said to his father that his brother spent all of his money on prostitutes, but how would he know that? Did his arrogance just lead him to assume? What assumptions do we make about those whom we've relegated to the Naughty List? How do we determine that they deserved to be on it, and do we "check it twice" for opportunities to bless or excuses to curse?

I don't have an earthly brother, but I have identified with the spiteful brother from time to time when evaluating my spiritual brothers. I don't have a flashy testimony. I was a well-behaved kid who grew up in a good home and started going to youth groups as a teenager, then eventually decided to commit myself to Jesus and his teachings. I never got into trouble and always lived on the straight and narrow path, but with that narrow living developed a narrow mind. I was resentful when others made what I believed to be immoral choices yet seemed to be rewarded, and I grew envious of those who had what I thought I deserved because, like the other brother, I "lived my life right." I was *covetous*, but I called it *righteous indignation.*

I can't pretend that indignation doesn't still flair up now and then, but these days I try to focus on gratitude. It's hard to covet when you're busy being grateful for what you have, yourself. According to God's Law, we all deserve to be on the "Naughty List," but Grace puts us on the Nice List, instead – that's why Grace is called a *gift,* and it's one gift we don't have to wait for Christmas to give to others.

JOURNAL QUESTIONS
- What areas do you struggle to feel superior to others? In what areas do you struggle to feel inferior?
- What are some practical ways to practice gratitude?

~ 17 ~
SCROOGE

"I don't deserve to be so happy. I can't help it;
I just can't help it."

Year: 1951
Distributor: Renown Pictures
Producer: Brian Desmond Hurst
Director: Brian Desmond Hurst
Writer: Noel Langley, based on the book by Charles Dickens
Runtime: 86 minutes
Rating: Approved

Scripture Reading: Acts 9:1-18

With so many adaptations of *A Christmas Carol* in circulation, it's difficult to choose. For my money, if I could only ever watch one version of the story it would be Alastair Sim's. Sim is the perfect Scrooge; whereas many others play him as an over-the-top grouch, Sim gives the character range and nuance, combining an unapproachable gruffness with gallows humor and smugness. His redemption feels totally earned and his exuberance appears completely authentic.

There is no way to overstate the importance of this story's impact on Christmas. It reinvigorated enthusiasm for the holiday when both society and the church had begun to distance themselves from it.[1] Charles Dickens believed that a renewed interest in Christmas would bolster community and provide a balm to a culture ravaged with poverty. He had a pregnant wife and counted on his book to provide the funds for his expanding family, yet, as a result of his prior novel failing to succeed, his publisher was skeptical of the project. Dickens was so sure of his work that he took a gamble and basically self-published it. Sadly, in spite of critical acclaim and the legacy it left, it made little money and he saw it as a disappointment. The irony is that *A Christmas Carol* went on to become the father of all "holiday specials." It is so powerful that *Scrooge* has become a synonym for *stingy* and the name *Ebenezer*, a biblical word that means *stone of help*, is forever associated with the book's miser.

The 1951 adaptation is particularly unique, deviating a little from the source material and embellishing the tale to give Scrooge an expanded origin. Thanks to this version, we see the steps Scrooge took in his descent into the "retching, grasping, scraping, covetous old sinner" that we meet in the beginning of the film. We see his anguish over watching his sister die having given birth to his nephew and the guilt of his broken promise to raise him. This film also gives Scrooge the last word when his fianceé (named Alice in this version) ends their engagement, assuring her that he *will* be happy in the life he's chosen. The scene was later parodied in the Bill Murray spoof, *Scrooged.*

The biggest change from the source material is with the Ghost of Christmas Present. In the book, the Spirits of Christmas Present are born, live, and die over the course of Christmas each year. Here, the Ghost of Christmas Present says, "Mortal! We Spirits of Christmas do not live only one day of our year. We live the whole three-hundred and sixty-five. So is it true of the Child born in Bethlehem. He does not live in men's hearts one day of the year, but in all days of the year." The line brings us to the spiritual root of the story; salvation. Even the Ghost of Christmas Past directly says as much. Modern versions tend to focus on charity and community, which are important but not the point. Charity is a *biproduct* of a transformed mind; it isn't about a change in holiday habits but a radical change in attitude.

There are two dynamics at work with repentance: the personal and the social. An average person who makes a life-changing commitment to Christ might face skepticism and even opposition from others, but Ebenezer isn't average; he's widely known (and despised). Such a public transformation must have been met with apprehension. We see glimpses of it with Mrs. Dilber but also experience acceptance when he visits his nephew.

The transformation of Scrooge reminds me of a man who was similarly hated named Saul. Saul was feared by the Christians of his time and was their chief villain, delighting in their deaths. A similarly dramatic encounter with Christ Himself changed his heart, and he became Paul, the author of most of the New Testament. I can only wonder what the process of acceptance was like for him. I bet some Christians were unhappy about their prime persecutor becoming their principal spokesman, but Jesus instructs us to pray for our enemies in Matthew 5:44. The consequence of such a prayer is the possibility of a transformation that seems as hard to believe as a ghost story.

JOURNAL QUESTIONS
- If you ever formally became a Christian, how did people in your life respond? Were they accepting or cautious?
- Have you ever known anyone who set out to change their ways whom you struggled to believe? Did the change stick?

~ 18 ~
A CHIPMUNK CHRISTMAS

"So that's what the spirit of Christmas means to you, Alvin? Buying presents for yourself?"

Year: 1981
Distributor: Bagdsarian Productions
Producer: Janice Karman, Ross Bagdasarian Jr.
Director: Phil Munroe
Writer: Janice Karman, Ross Bagdasarian Jr.
Runtime: 30 minutes
Rating: Not Rated

Scripture Reading: Mark 12:41-44

If you're like me, you were introduced to *Alvin and the Chipmunks* thanks to "The Chipmunk Song (Christmas Don't Be Late)," a novelty Christmas song concocted by the late Ross Bagdasarian. Ross built an empire of albums with the Chipmunks, singing all of the parts and then speeding up the voices up in editing. Several albums and a short-lived animated series followed, and they stayed popular enough to justify a Christmas special, no doubt hoping to capitalize on the notoriety of the title rodents' signature tune.

A Chipmunk Christmas opens by introducing us to Tommy, a sick little boy who idolizes Alvin and longs for a "Golden Echo" Harmonica, just like his hero's. It's a somber introduction and implies that Tommy is dying. His sister devotedly sits by his bed to read to him but knows that the only thing that can cure him would be the harmonica. We then cut to the Seville house, where Alvin and his brothers attempt to wake their foster father/producer/manager Dave so that they can go shopping. On one side of town is a trio of anthropomorphic chipmunk/children who just want to shop, but on the other is a little boy who just wants to live. Alvin learns about how serious Tommy's condition is and gives him his very own harmonica, a possession so prized he even has a little bed for it.

In *A Christmas Carol*, Dickens defines the season as a time "when Want is keenly felt, and Abundance rejoices." That disparity is beautifully illustrated here. The characters were designed by Chuck Jones, the director of the *Grinch* cartoon, and it shows in how expressive they are. Tommy's shift from illness to elation as he opens Alvin's present is palpable. After doing the noble thing, Alvin learns that he's expected to perform with his harmonica at Carnegie Hall on Christmas Eve, and he obsesses over how to raise the money to replace it. Dave, in turn, misinterprets Alvin's desperation as greed. The special ends with Alvin failing to earn enough, meaning that the concert will be ruined, but he's happened upon by a kind, old woman who insists on buying him the harmonica as a gift. What strikes me is that Alvin's sorrow isn't over his harmonica but because he thinks that he's let everyone down. The kind woman's act doesn't just replace a trinket but saves the concert. Tommy, fully healed, is able to go, too. All he'd wanted was a harmonica, but he got to be on stage with his hero as well! Like Alvin, we never know just how far even our smallest acts of kindness go, and, like Tommy, we can never predict just how great the blessings we receive can be.

A Chipmunk Christmas wonderfully communicates our reading today, in which Jesus notes the lavish donations of rich temple-goers versus the mere cents given by a widow. He asserts that her offering, though less, means much more than the larger gifts of the others because they're giving out of their abundance while she gives from what little she has.

The kind woman at the end of the special who gives Alvin his new harmonica is none other than Mrs. Claus. As a character who rarely gets the spotlight, it makes the scene so much more meaningful than if Santa had given it to him, much like the widow's offering meant more, though it was less. Thanks to this show, as a kid I believed that while Santa was out on his sleigh Mrs. Claus gave in more personal ways. In fact, one of my most treasured gifts was from "Mrs. Claus," who fixed a stuffed dog I sent with my letter to the North Pole, similar to Bee Bee, the bear I discussed in the Introduction. It's hard to recall each individual gift "Santa" gave me, but I'll never forget the one from Mrs. Claus.

As we celebrate a season of charity, it's important to remember the difference between *giving* and *sacrifice*. Giving is from our abundance, sacrifice costs us. Having learned of Tommy's predicament, Alvin could have had a fundraiser to buy him a harmonica but offered his own instead. And just as Alvin got to play a song for Mrs. Claus on the harmonica she gave him, we receive indescribable blessings when we are willing to surrender our "Golden Echo" Harmonicas to help the Tommy's of the world. Yours, like the widow's, may not seem like much, but the value of true sacrifice is priceless.

JOURNAL QUESTIONS

- What has been a "Golden Echo Harmonica" in your life?
- Have you ever given in a way that put you out? In what ways were you blessed for your generosity?

~ 19 ~
THE LITTLE DRUMMER BOY

"It is not necessary that you understand.
Go to him."

Year: 1968
Distributor: Anderson Digital
Producers: Jules Bass, Arthur Rankin Jr.
Directors: Jules Bass, Arthur Rankin Jr.
Writer: Romero Muller
Runtime: 25 minutes
Rating: Not Rated

Scripture Reading: Colossians 3:22-24

If I were to ask you about your favorite Christmas carols, chances are that "The Little Drummer Boy" would be somewhere on your Top Ten list. One of the great strengths of the Rankin/Bass specials was their ability to expand on a beloved song of the season to create a story. Our short today does just that, combining the story of the First Christmas with that of the fictional hero of the title song, a child who hates humanity because of his parents' death.

The Little Drummer Boy is one of the few Christmas specials that's both mainstream and spiritual. We only meet the Holy Family at the end and never see the infant Jesus, which gives a lot of weight to the exchange between him and the drummer boy. Instead, the film focuses on the drummer boy, named Aaron, and his pet camel, donkey, and lamb. In the beginning of the film, they're snatched by Ben Haramed, a street performer who exploits Aaron's musical gifts in a similar way to how Stromboli uses Pinocchio. We then meet the Three Kings on their journey to Bethlehem.

Aaron was once a shepherd whose family was killed by bandits who burned down their farm. All that Aaron has left is his drum, the final gift from his father, as well as his three animal companions. Ben sells the camel to the Three Kings, making Aaron even more alone. He escapes, but his lamb is run over by a chariot and nearly dies. Grief-stricken, Aaron finds the Kings, who suggest that he bring his lamb to the infant whom they've come to pay homage to. Feeling a need to offer the newborn a gift, Aaron plays his drum with all his might and the Child Christ is pleased; the lamb is healed, sponging away the hate inside of Aaron's heart.

Rankin/Bass specials have low production value. The plots are thin and the stop motion is always basic. Even so, there's a lot of heart in today's special. The drama of Aaron losing his family and then almost losing his lamb is fairly intense for a kids' show. Additionally, while the songs are forgettable (in fact, Ben's song has been heavily edited out of recent broadcasts for being ethnically insensitive), there are other musical pieces which are haunting. It seems as if more effort went into this production than some of their others, just as the drummer boy played his best for the baby Jesus.

That said, *The Little Drummer Boy* is problematic in a few regards. As a Christian, I am delighted whenever I find a thoughtful, spiritual holiday special that acknowledges the religious meaning of Christmas while also managing to be entertaining. That's a difficult balance. On the other hand, there's no such a character as the Little Drummer Boy in the bible, nor can we be sure as to how many kings there were or, for that matter, if they were kings. Or, further expanding on the mystery, when they actually visited Jesus. Stories like this, enjoyable as they may be, go a long way to continue the fictionalization of Christmas. If I can use a wooden stable to represent what historical evidence says was most likely a cave and surround it with Three Kings who were more than likely just a group of Zoroastrian star-gazers who came two years later and call *that* Christmas, at what point do the angels and the virgin birth become negotiable too?

In its defense, *The Little Drummer Boy* isn't a story about Jesus, it's about a hurting child and how encountering Christ can change your life. It's the story of someone who, thinking he had nothing to offer the Lord, found that he had a wonderful gift to give because he offered that gift in excellence. It might not be *correct*, but that doesn't make it *false*. Our passage today reminds us to be like the Little Drummer Boy, doing everything we do with all of our heart as if doing it for the Lord and not for people. That task can be especially challenging given the Ben Harameds running around, stealing our joy or making our life miserable. Still, if we can muster the strength to play our best, whatever our "drums" may be for us individually, then the reward will be far greater than the gift we ourselves can give.

JOURNAL QUESTIONS

- What activities are hard to do "as if working" for the Lord? How can we change out outlook on those activities?
- What are some non-biblical Christmas traditions that make you feel closer to God?

~ 20 ~
HOW THE GRINCH STOLE CHRISTMAS

"He puzzled and puzzed till his puzzler was sore. Then the Grinch thought of something he hadn't before. Maybe Christmas, he thought, doesn't come from a store. Maybe Christmas, perhaps, means a little bit more."

Year: 1966
Distributor: Warner Bros. Television
Producers: Chuck Jones, Ted Geisel
Directors: Chuck Jones, Ben Washam
Writer: Irv Spector, Bob Ogle, based on the book by Dr. Seuss
Runtime: 26 minutes
Rating: Unrated

Scripture Reading: 1 Peter 3:8-12

While a lot of people might prefer the live-action 2000 film starring Jim Carrey, for me there's nothing quite like the classic cartoon by acclaimed animator Chuck Jones. The short perfectly realizes the simplicity of Dr. Seuss' book, with the indelible voice of Thurl Ravenscroft singing "You're a Mean One, Mister Grinch" as the titular grouch attempts to rob Whoville of its seasonal joy. The live-action version attempts to rationalize the Grinch's nastiness by giving him a backstory, but the cartoon and book see no need to make him sympathetic; he's nothing but a bitter hermit who hates Christmas because, to him, it's all noise. To hear him explain the Whos' festivities it's easy to see why he feels that way! Every toy he lists is a progressively louder sound machine, and the town anthem is gibberish. Can you really blame him for being a bit grumpy?

The Grinch decides to "steal" Christmas, which, to him, means taking away those trappings. He steals their gifts and decorations, he even takes their furniture and food! He's out of control as his pent-up frustrations manifest in the form of a crime spree through town. Then, as he prepares to chuck the Whos' stuff into an abyss, the townspeople gather around and sing anyway. The Grinch cannot screw his head around it; he thought this would stop the noise but finally comes to the conclusion that Christmas isn't gifts and tinsel. It isn't noise at all. He couldn't understand it before because it wasn't a *head* problem – it was a *heart* problem.

I had a "heart problem" when a friend joined me for a trip to a church in the Keys where I was invited to preach.

We took her car, and she drove. It was her prerogative as the driver to control the radio, but unfortunately one area we couldn't be any more different is in our musical tastes. I like classic rock, 80's metal, and electronic; she likes country and rap. That seven hour drive was like seven *days*. I felt like the Grinch by the time we arrived, slumped over in my seat with imaginary drumsticks bludgeoning my eardrums with all the noise...noise...noise...NOISE!!!

My friend isn't a churchgoer and wasn't planning on attending the services I was preaching. Then, after a couple from the church had us over for dinner she had a change of heart and decided to come. I was so happy to have her there, and she ended up having a surprisingly good time. When we set out for the sojourn home the following morning, I sank into my seat, gearing up for another seven hours of noise, but she surprised me. Something pleasant came out of the radio. Something *familiar*. After a few notes I recognized it – a new, electronic cover of one of my favorite 80's songs! I shot up in my seat and fixed my hair like I was meeting a blind date. Granted, the rest of the trip was rap and country but I was in such good spirits that I didn't mind. And you know, some of it even started to grow on me. *Some* if it.

Not everyone will make the effort, just as some will

dismiss the Whos in their life because of the "noise." That noise might be actual noise from literal noisy neighbors or just the opinions of people we don't like or agree with. The Whos in the cartoon may have been terrible neighbors, but that doesn't excuse the Grinch from robbing them anymore than scripture lets us off the hook for stealing someone's joy or telling them how to live just because they offend us.

Peter says in today's scripture to repay offenses with blessing, not insult. One of the ways we can do that is by actually making an effort to *listen* and not just *hear.* There's a difference between the two. Maybe things won't improve between you and your Whos, but if we make an effort to listen past the noise, we might just discover a new "song" that we like, and every so often they might even surprise us with a familiar tune that we have in common and can sing together.

JOURNAL QUESTIONS
- Who are the Whos in your life that you struggle to "hear?"
- Have you ever found that you appreciated something that you never thought you would once you tried it?

~ 21 ~
THE SANTA CLAUSE

"You see, children hold the spirit of Christmas within their hearts. You don't wanna be responsible for killing the spirit of Christmas, now would you...Santa?"

Year: 1994
Distributor: Buena Vista Pictures
Producers: Robert Newmyer, Brian Reilly, Jeffrey Silver
Director: John Pasquin
Writers: Leo Benevenuti and Steve Rudnick
Runtime: 97 minutes
Rating: PG

Scripture Reading: Jonah 1:1-17

The first in an eventual trilogy, *The Santa Clause* is the story of Scott Calvin, an ad exec for a toy company who is trying to connect with his son over Christmas. Hearing a man on the roof, Scott startles Santa, who falls to his death. Scott becomes the new Santa but spends the better part of the film trying to hide from his destiny and prove his sanity so that he doesn't lose visitation rights to see his son.

Compared with its sequels, *The Santa Clause* is dark and even a bit cynical. Consider how blasé the scene of Scott scaring Santa literally to death is and the subsequent banter with his son. Furthermore, when Scott and Charlie arrive at the North Pole and meet Bernard, the head elf seems more annoyed than upset. *Santa's dead, there's a new Santa, move on.* There's no scene whatsoever to show any kind of sadness for the previous Santa. There is no loving tribute. Even Scott sort of takes in stride that he indirectly killed a man. What about that Santa? How long had he been in the suit? Did he have a "Charlie" of his own somewhere waiting for an elf to come bring him a folded Christmas tree skirt? Did he have a Mrs. Claus? The sequel says that's a requirement, so what of her? Was she sent back to the mortal realm? Did she blink out of existence like her husband? I presume Disney didn't want the movie to dwell on such morbid things as it might be upsetting to younger viewers, but omitting those answers and emotions makes the film feel cold.

Another curious choice is that the film doesn't bring Scott and his ex-wife Laura back together. Usually, in films of this sort, when a dad is in competition with an unlikable stepdad over his child's love the dad and the mom get back together and the child is all the happier. It doesn't help that

Judge Reinhold, who is doomed to be insufferable in every Christmas movie from *Clause* to *Gremlins*, never gets any redemption; the psychiatrist is just as annoying at the end of the movie as he is at the beginning. Still, he'd likely argue that not getting Scott and Laura back together is a healthier way for a Christmas movie to end. With so many blended families, children need movies like this more than ones that reinforce the idea that parents always reunite, because the reality is that they often do not. Much of this film is about coming to terms with reality. For example, a significant portion of the film's run-time focuses on Scott denying and running away from his responsibilities as Santa rather than facing the truth. It reminds me of another man who ran from his destiny, a prophet named Jonah.

The story of Jonah is as fantastical to some readers as Santa is. Jonah is told by God to preach to the people of Ninevah, but because he was bigoted against them he refuses and runs the other way. Calamity ensues; a ship he is on nearly capsizes, and when they realize that it's the wrath of Jonah's God which has brought the tumult on their boat he lets them throw him overboard. Jonah is then gobbled up by a gigantic fish. In the fish's belly, Jonah realizes the futility of running away from God and is at his lowest point. To his astonishment, the fish then spits him out onto the shores of Ninevah. Filled with gratitude, Jonah proclaims the Word of God to the people and they're spared! Yet, the book ends on a curious note. Even though he now sees the importance of surrendering to God's will, Jonah is still unmoved towards Ninevah and is *angry* that its people are going to be saved! The story concludes with Jonah wishing that he were dead and God essentially telling him to get over himself.

When God lays something on our hearts for us to do that we don't necessary want to, it usually won't be as much fun as becoming Santa Claus. And, just like the end of this film, things might not always go the way we expect or hope for just because we surrendered to God's will. The film says that seeing is not believing but that believing is seeing. We can fail to recognize the potential in others whom we don't "believe in," but God can use us to do amazing things for the Ninevites in our life if we are willing to peer beyond that disbelief and allow ourselves to *see* them. He can even help us see our own potential and believe in ourselves.

JOURNAL QUESTIONS
- Has God led you to do something you've run from?
- How can we love past our prejudices and have God's heart for all people?

~ 22 ~
RUDOLPH THE RED-NOSED REINDEER

"Rudolph, with your nose so bright, won't you guide my sleigh tonight?"

Year: 1964
Distributor: Classic Media
Producers: Jules Bass and Arthur Rankin Jr.
Director: Larry Roemer
Writer: Romeo Muller, from a story by Robert May based on the song by Johnny Marks
Runtime: 47 minutes
Rating: TV-G

Scripture Reading: 1 Corinthians 12:12-26

The flagship of the classic Rankin/Bass Christmas specials, *Rudolph the Red-Nosed Reindeer* puts a story to a classic carol about a reindeer who is ostracized for having a peculiarly red and shiny nose but discovers that Santa needs his help to guide his sleigh during a blizzard. During his adventures, Rudolph meets an elf who wants to be a dentist, an absent-minded prospector, and an island of toys that were abandoned just because they were misfits.

Everyone has a favorite Santa; mine is David "The Big Lebowski" Huddleston, followed by Douglas Seale. That being said, I imagine everyone also has a *least* favorite, and mine, hands down, is this Santa. Honestly, everyone in this North Pole is contemptible. Santa's Head Elf is a vicious blowhard; Rudolph's father, Donner, forces him to hide his nose from others like a leper; and then there's Santa himself, who flippantly rejects Rudolph over his nose, telling Donner that he should *feel ashamed* of himself for having a son like him! He doesn't even want to make time for a song that his elves prepared *in his honor* and criticizes it when he hears it. This Santa is so petty that I've wondered if when he had the misfit toys jump out of the sleigh at the end of the show he wasn't just dumping them into the ocean.

Additionally, I was always baffled as to why Hermey was treated so shamefully. The idea that the elves don't do anything but make toys doesn't work. Surely there has to be elves who clean Santa's colorless, gray castle. Certainly there are elves who cook or make the clothes or tend the animals. There is an elf doctor in *The Year Without a Santa Claus* (going back to my Rankin/Bass "shared universe" theory), so why wouldn't there be an elf dentist?

All joking aside, it's not hard to see why this film is a

classic. Musical numbers by Burl Ives, memorable characters like Yukon and the Snow Bumble, and a story about fitting in invite us back year after year. We might not know what it is like to have a glowing red nose, but most of us can relate to the desire to belong. Fred Rogers said "we human beings all want to know that we're acceptable, that our being alive somehow makes a difference in the lives of others."[1] I would bet that applies to elves and reindeer, too. We want to feel like we belong and have something to contribute. Take, for instance, Hermey's knowledge of tooth extraction, which saves Rudolph, his parents, and Clarice from the Bumble. And, of course, we all know about how Rudolph's nose, a source of ridicule, was the very thing that saved Christmas. Every one of us has something that either people have made us feel ashamed of or that we keep hidden like Rudolph's nose for fear of judgment. Our scripture today discusses this and gives us comfort to know that our "shameful" parts are actually our most precious.

1 Corinthians 12 is a difficult chapter at a glance. It describes the church as the Body of Christ, saying that each one of us is part of a greater whole and that every one of us has something to offer. In verses 22-24, Paul postulates that the "parts", that is to say persons, who seem the weakest, or

even shameful, deserve special honor; those who appear to be the most replaceable are *indispensable*. I think the same thing can be said about our individual bodies and our own red noses. What you see in yourself as a defect is what makes you exceptional. As Clarice says to Rudolph, the red of our nose is "what makes it so grand."

As we play the reindeer games of life, we should look for who to invite, not who to exclude. It's *easy* to overlook others who are different but that doesn't make it *right*. It's also important to guard our hearts from becoming bitter towards those who judge us for our noses but don't appear to have red noses of their own. We all have them, but some of us are like Donner and know how to cover them better. So wear your nose boldly and blaze a path. Your light might be the only thing than can get through someone's storm.

JOURNAL QUESTIONS
- What aspects of yourself have you either felt a need to hide or have been ridiculed over?
- How can you use your insecurities to bring God glory?

~ 23 ~
HOME ALONE

"You can be too old for a lot of things, but
you're never too old to be afraid."

Year: 1990
Distributor: 20th Century Fox
Producer: John Hughes
Director: Chris Columbus
Writer: John Hughes
Runtime: 103 minutes
Rating: PG

Scripture Reading: Matthew 6:25-34

Kevin McCallister is accidentally left home by his family, who have gone on a trip to Paris. Alone, he wards off a pair of burglars called the Wet Bandits by booby-trapping his house while learning to appreciate his family. It's a seasonal classic which inspired a slew of copycats and was directed by Chris Columbus, the writer of *Gremlins* (my favorite Christmas movie), and was written by John Hughes, who also wrote *National Lampoon's Christmas Vacation* and the remake of *Miracle on 34th Street.*

In the chapter on *The Town Santa Forgot*, I told you about "Jeremy," a boy from a youth group where I served as a volunteer. During the annual Rock the Universe event, he ran off at Universal Studios and I had to find him. He was the only youth in my experience to ever run off during the event, but he certainly wasn't the only misplaced one.

Years later, I was a Youth Pastor with a group of my own. I'd been serving at a particular church for about seven years and had taken my group to Rock the Universe many times. In what would be my last Rock the Universe with that group, one of our boys, not much older than Kevin in the film, got lost. Saturday always concludes with a message and candle lighting ceremony, which I required all of our Youth to attend. With almost two hours left before the park closed, they wanted to see more attractions - especially the Harry Potter section that just opened. After about thirty minutes of exploring Diagon Alley, we left and realized that our own "Kevin" wasn't among us. We looked everywhere for Kevin, traversing the crooked streets of the Potter replica, but could not find him. Like the scene where Kevin's sister counts the neighbor thinking that it's him, each of us was sure that our Kevin had been with us. Eventually, we realized that we had lost him at the concert.

Now, most Youth Workers might have panicked at this point. My volunteers certainly did. Not me. I was a pro at losing Youth. In fact, I was patting myself on the back for having only lost one of them. My volunteers were less than impressed, though. They were like a gaggle of Kevin's moms, all very frantic. It was nearing the end of the event and was after midnight. Everyone was tired, sore, and hungry. Well, I wasn't. As Youth Pastor, I was having a *very* different evening than everyone else. Having managed several conflicts, if I'd been any frostier Santa might have come to take me up to the North Pole.

Security was funneling everyone out, so we decided that we'd probably find him along the way. Kevin was there by the exit, white as a sheet and shaking. Not unlike Kevin and his mom, he and I stared at each other for a moment. Kevin was a good kid, more afraid that I would be upset with him than being upset with me for losing him. I wasn't upset, of course. We hugged, and I assured him that I was glad he was okay.

Kevin was smart enough to deduce that we'd have to leave eventually, so, rather than looking for us, he walked to the exit and waited. As my Youth Staff and I roved the park in search of him, some of us more anxious than others, he was there all along. It reminds me a lot of the ending of our film today. Kevin's mom, played by Catherine O'Hara, was desperate to get home, but, for all of the hoops she jumped through, she arrived when the rest of the McCallisters did. It worked out, just the same; no amount of worrying made it any better for her than it did for my Youth Team and our own Kevin, or any of us for the innumerable things that we worry about on a daily basis.

In our passage, Jesus makes the potent point that we can't add to our life by worrying. If anything, we take away from it. As it says in Romans 8:28, all things work for the good of those who love the Lord. Had they not left Kevin behind, their house would have been robbed. That's not to excuse stranding him, but a lot of inexcusable things happen to us. We can either ride along in a box truck of worry with Kevin's mom and accomplish nothing or we can prepare for the Wet Bandits of life like Kevin and safeguard the house that is our mind against despairing them.

JOURNAL QUESTIONS
- What do you find yourself worrying about most?
- What positive actions can you take against worry?

~ 24 ~
A CHARLIE BROWN CHRISTMAS

"I guess you were right, Linus. I shouldn't have picked this little tree. Everything I do turns into a disaster. I guess I really don't know what Christmas is all about. Isn't there anyone who knows what Christmas is all about?"

Year: 1965
Distributor: 20th Century Fox Home Entertainment
Producer: Bill Melendez
Director: Bill Melendez
Writer: Charles M. Schultz
Runtime: 25 minutes
Rating: TV-G

Scripture Reading: Luke 2:8-14

A Charlie Brown Christmas accurately captures the feeling of reading the comic strip, with an episodic focus on exchanges between characters rather than on the overarching narrative. Still, weaving through the moments is a solid story about a sad, lonely boy who searches for the true meaning of Christmas in an aluminum, commercial world. Charlie seeks help from his "friend" Lucy, who, despite always being mean to him, cares enough to offer him the cogent advice that if he's feeling disconnected he should go out and find a way of getting involved. Lucy convinces him to direct their school's Christmas play, but his classmates have little to no interest in following his leadership.

At the time of its release, the network anticipated *A Charlie Brown Christmas* was going to be a flop. It's a slow-paced, plodding piece with jazz before jazz was associated with Christmas (and only is today thanks to the success of this special). It has heavy religious themes, and not even a laugh track to cue viewers in as to when they should react to the subtle humor. Yet, the Peanuts gang earned the second highest ratings the night it debuted and is played every year. For a rushed, six month production made on a shoestring budget, its impact is as remarkable as Charlie's humble tree.

One thing that keeps us coming back to *A Charlie Brown Christmas* is that it's brave enough to do something that most specials won't: admit Christmas is an emotionally confusing – and even sad – time for many. The very holiday specials that we return to often reinforce our internalized notion that Christmas is supposed to be a time for family and togetherness, but not everyone has that. These reminders of what society says we *ought* to have can make us feel even worse. Sometimes, we only have Christmas because *we* make the magic happen for ourselves, and there's nothing wrong with that. In fact, making that effort can be the very thing that helps us shake our seasonal blues.

I was 15 and it didn't look like my family was going to be doing much celebrating. My dad was transferred and we had to sell our house, the first my parents ever bought. Worse, the Realtor told us not to decorate because it might be offensive to some buyers. We are festive people and always go all out, so by mid-December I couldn't take it anymore. In a weirdly positive act of teenage defiance, I decided that if my parents weren't going to "do" Christmas, I would. I went to K-Mart, where decorations were on sale. For about $50, I turned my room into a wonderland ($50 went farther back then). My parents were moved, enough to snap them out of their funk and decorate as usual. Not to sound dramatic, but I like to think I saved Christmas that year.

In preparing for this book, I talked with my parents about it. They didn't remember the sadness, only the happy memories made after. This prompted my mom to take out our old home movies for the first time in years, and she discovered a surprise; we recorded my decorations on our camcorder! Seeing that VHS brought me right back there. Reminiscing over past holidays made this one even brighter. In 1997 I was just a 15 year old who wanted Christmas, I had no idea my effort would make a difference two decades later. Similarly, we can't know just how fruitful our efforts will be unless we try.

Christmas is like a dream that we have the power to pull out of ourselves, into reality, and invite others to join. For Christians, the dream of salvation was born into reality in that stable – the hope of peace on earth and good will to others. Jesus said that peacemakers are blessed to be called God's children, but peace is like Christmas: it doesn't just "happen," we have to make it happen. And just like Linus' blanket and a little love was all it took to help those shallow classmates see the beauty in Charlie Brown's small, frail tree, our authenticity can inspire others when we make the effort to show them what Christmas is all about.

JOURNAL QUESTIONS
- How can we be peacemakers at Christmastime?
- Have you ever seen the beauty in someone or something that others couldn't? Has anyone seen it in you?

~ 25 ~
A CHRISTMAS STORY

"You'll shoot your eye out, kid."

Year: 1983
Distributor: MGM/UA Entertainment Co.
Producers: Rene Dupont, Bob Clark
Director: Bob Clark
Writers: Jean Shepherd (based on his novel), Leigh Brown, and Bob Clark
Runtime: 94 minutes
Rating: PG

Scripture Reading: James 4:2-3

It's hard to imagine that *A Christmas Story*, possibly the single most-watched holiday film of all time (in no small part due to TBS playing it 12 times a day on December 25th) was made by the director of the festive holiday horror *Black Christmas*, as well as flicks like *Porky's* and *Baby Geniuses*. Siskel and Ebert, upon the film's release, were astonished to have enjoyed it, given their hatred for director Bob Clark's other work.[1] It just goes to show the power of expectations.

The movie is about expectation and disappointment. Early in the film, Old Man Parker is excited over winning a "major award" without any idea of what it is. When a crate's wheeled in like the monolith from *2001: A Space Odyssey*, the "award" is revealed to be a lamp shaped like a woman's leg, but the Old Man makes the most of it, just happy to have won something. He also anticipates his annual turkey dinner, only to have it gobbled up by the neighbors' 785 smelly hound dogs. Ralphie waits for his *Annie* decoder but is disappointed to discover that all it decodes are Ovaltine ads. And, of course, there's his beloved Red Ryder Carbine Action 200-shot Range Model air rifle.

Throughout the film, Ralphie plots and maneuvers to convince his parents that he should have it, but everyone (even "Santa") tells him that he'll just shoot his eye out if he gets it. At long last, Christmas comes. It seems like Ralphie isn't getting his Red Ryder, but, lo and behold, it's behind a desk as one final surprise! And, just like everybody warned, Ralphie almost shoots his eye out.

I didn't see the film until I was an adult working at Blockbuster Video. We were open on holidays but had very few customers on Christmas Day. I can think of maybe two. There was a trailer tape that had to be on constantly, but for

Christmas my manager decided to play *A Christmas Story*. I stood behind the counter and saw the whole thing with nary a customer. My reaction was a rousing "Okay?" As if I was a character from the film, my built-up expectations turned to disappointment.

Then again, what *could* have lived up to the hype? I was expecting the best Christmas movie ever, one that would become the flagship of my holiday viewing traditions for the next decade – a film worthy of playing for 24 straight hours. Like Ralphie having searched under the tree but not finding what I anticipated, I never watched it again until working on this book. I actually appreciated it more now, having seen it for what it is and not for what it was made out to be.

Despite being set in the 30s/40s, the movie captures a sense of childhood that applies to all of us. Watching it, I remember the daydreams I had to pass the time at school. I remember being in trouble the first time I said a bad word in front of my dad (I've never cursed in front of him since). Most of all, I remember the disappointment of unfulfilled expectations.

If you're using this book as a December devotional, chances are you're reading this on Christmas Day (is there a better day for this one?). You may have opened your presents already, or not. You may have wanted something as badly as Ralphie wanted his gun, or maybe not. Even so, you know what it's like to *want*, to long for something and not receive it. A Ralphie-like part of us might even be tempted to look past everything else waiting for us under life's tree in our mad search for the one thing we're looking for. And there *is* another present for you. You can't see it, but it's beautiful, and its freshly wrapped with each new morning. You can't hold it, but it's priceless: It's *contentment;* a quizzing glass that helps us examine our hearts and motives, and focus on gratitude for what we have. The movie ends with the Parkers going to a Chinese restaurant. They're introduced to Chinese turkey (duck) and celebrate a Christmas that they will never forget, showing us that just because things don't always go the way we *hope* it doesn't mean that things can't be *great.*

JOURNAL QUESTIONS

- What was a "Red Ryder" present for you as a kid? Did you get your dream gift? If so, do you appreciate it now?
- Have you ever had a Christmas when everything seemed to go wrong but turned out better than you ever expected?

~ 26 ~
MICKEY'S ONCE UPON A CHRISTMAS

"It'll be another 356 days until we get more Christmas."

Year: 1999
Distributor: Walt Disney Home Video
Producer: Sherri Stringfellow
Directors: June Falkenstein, Alex Mann, Bradley Raymond, Toby Shelton, Bill Speers
Writers: Charlie Cohen, Scott Spencer Gordon, Tom Nance, Carter Crocker, Richard Cray, Temple Matthews, Thomas Hart, Eddie Guzelian, Alex Mann
Runtime: 66 minutes
Rating: Not Rated

Scripture Reading: Acts 20:33-35

A Day-After-Christmas bonus! While all the shorts on this video are great, for our purposes I want to focus on the first one, *Stuck on Christmas*. Huey, Dewey, and Louie blast through Christmas, dazzled by gifts and acting rudely toward Donald, Daisy, and Uncle Scrooge. When the day is over, they kneel at their window and wish upon a star that it could be Christmas every day; they get their wish, but not quite how they meant it.

The following morning isn't *another* Christmas: it's the *same one.* Happy to have it again, and already knowing how it will go, they run to their presents and tear through the day with even less regard for others than they had to begin with. Soon, it's obvious that they're stuck in a loop of some sort, not unlike the Bill Murray film, *Groundhog Day.* It seems that they'll be trapped in that Christmas forever, so it doesn't take long for the novelty to wear off. Soon, they grow apathetic – they're tired of the turkey; they're bored of their gifts. Finally, the boys read the card that came with their toys, which they've overlooked every time, reminding them that family, not gifts, is what make Christmas special. Realizing how shamefully they've behaved, the boys decide to make the next day the best Christmas possible for their family and not just for themselves. In so doing, the loop is broken and life finally moves forward.

There are a lot of Christmas movies, but nothing for the day after, which is ironic given how many specials have a sentiment about keeping the spirit all year. If you've been using this book as an Advent devotional, then today would be the day after Christmas. You might be feeling a variety of emotions. Maybe you're glad that it's over and look forward to the New Year, or perhaps, like Huey, Dewey, and Louie, you're wishing it could go on forever. If that's you, then you will be happy to know that Christmas isn't *technically* over. Advent, the fancy word for the Christmas season, doesn't end until the first Sunday after New Years Day, which is called Epiphany. Epiphany is when we observe the visit of the Wise Men, officially concluding the season.

You don't have to wait that long for more Christmas, however. Many of our neighbors around the globe have an extra holiday on December 26 called Boxing Day. No, it's not the day that we box up our presents and decorations, it's a day dating back to the Middle Ages when nobleman would offer Christmas boxes (small gifts, money, or food) to their servants. Today, it's a time of honoring those in the service professions, like postal workers. Maybe the evil mailman in *Olive, the Other Reindeer* would have cooled his jets if he had been given a Christmas Box? Boxing Day is special for an additional reason; it shares a date with the Feast Day of St. Stephen in Catholicism.

The Apostles were struggling to fulfill their mission of spreading the Gospel because they were overwhelmed by distributing food to the needy, so they appointed Stephen to take over those duties. He was a great man who performed miracles and did a lot of good, but he was falsely accused of blasphemy by the Jewish High Council. They stoned him to death, making him the first Christian martyr.

It's fitting that the day many countries choose to lift up those who serve others would also be the day we celebrate a man whose only crime was his dedication to serving. Many of us can relate to Huey, Dewey, and Louie's enthusiasm – and maybe even their apathy. When Christmas is nothing but making ourselves merry, even the heaviest box under the tree feels hollow eventually. As our passage points out, it's more blessed to give than to get, so if you feel trapped in a loop of routine, you might find freedom in serving. We can enjoy Christmas every single day, not by rehearsing the same rhythms over and over again like Huey, Dewey, and Louie but by hoisting Santa's bag onto our shoulders and going out into the cold night with the hope of offering just a little warmth.

JOURNAL QUESTIONS

- What are some ways to keep the Christmas spirit all year?
- Who do you know in the service industry who could use a little extra loving care this time of the year?

~ IN ~
CLOSING

"Christmas is not a time nor a season, but a
state of mind. To cherish peace and goodwill, to
be plenteous in mercy, is to have the
real spirit of Christmas."

Calvin Coolidge

In the previous chapter, I asked you what are some
ways of keeping the spirit of Christmas all year. I've asked
you a lot of questions over the course of this journey, and
now I'd like to conclude this book by sharing an answer of
my own and by asking a more pointed question:

Is there a rule that says it has to be once a year?

We pack up so much into our totes and our trunks after the season is over. We pack up the ornaments and the trees. We roll up the lights and put them away. The movies and CDs go back on the shelf, neglected for another year. As does the nativity and its infant Jesus figurine. Unfortunately, some of us pack the real Jesus up with it. Worst of all, we pack up the lessons that the season taught us. We trumpet "peace on earth and good will to men" from Thanksgiving to New Years Eve and then resume our regularly scheduled judgments.

I think that the reason so many Christmas specials talk about keeping the spirit all year is because deep down we really do want that. We want to show our loved ones how much we care, but for too many of us Christmas is the only time of the year in which it seems appropriate to express our feelings. Deep down we want to be silly, to act like kids, but we're too grown up and self-conscious. Worse, we allow the labels we identify with to keep us from loving our neighbors because we're afraid to be seen as supporting *their* labels.

So, a follow-up question: *What will it take for us to keep Christmas all year?* For you, does is it only feel like Christmas when we hear the songs or see the specials? Then listen to them and watch them! Maybe not every day, but what's wrong with popping *Rudolph* into the DVD player in March? Why not call up a Christmas station on Pandora while driving home from a stressful workday sometime in August? Why only read and study Luke 2 during the Advent season? Why not keep your nativity out on your shelf if you have a hard time keeping Jesus on your mind?

I'm reminded of a story that an older woman whom I am friends with told me about her experience with divorce. She was as devoted to her husband as she was to the Lord, but he didn't reciprocate. It was an abusive relationship, but she strained to recognize it at the time, too distracted by her false assertions that their marital failings were her fault for not being a good enough wife.

After the divorce, my friend struggled to find joy in her daily routines. Everything that she believed her life was and would be ended, and only her faith was there to hold her up. Her solace came in the form of a plate, a Christmas dinner plate. She ate dinner on that Christmas plate every night because she finally realized that, free of the abuse and free to build her life however she wanted, every day was now like a little Christmas.

My friend's story touched me deeply. So deeply, in fact, that it moved me to follow her example. My Christmas dishes are in the cupboard year-round, and every so often, as the mood strikes me, I'll use them. I have a small nativity, one with all the pieces glued in place, that I'll bring out now and then. I even have a small, decorated table top tree that I put up when I "need a little Christmas."

But here's the thing about the tree and the songs and the dishes. Those accoutrements help to give us the *feeling* of Christmas, but that's not the same as having the *spirit*. To have the spirit of Christmas is a change in attitude. It is the willingness to find excuses to show others you love them. It takes being thoughtful, and it takes stepping aside from our self-consciousness and allowing ourselves the freedom to be frivolous. Most importantly, having the spirit of Christmas is to have a heart for giving and for serving. Our nativities and our faith shouldn't merely be a display; we must go and *live* them. Jesus didn't stay in the manger. Neither can we.

~ NOTES ~

CHAPTER 4
  1.) Wonderful resources for pastors who struggle with burnout can be found at: *www.pastorburnout.com*

CHAPTER 10
  1.) The Blu-Ray features discuss this if you have it, but otherwise here is a great article about it in Forbes: *https://www.forbes.com/sites/scottmendelson/2013/12/25/ when-superman-became-santa-claus/#3cf6e2e18ef5*

CHAPTER 12
  1.) From *Wishful Thinking: A Seeker's ABC* (1993 expanded edition) by Frederick Buechner. Witty read with an everyman approach to making theology understandable, but with a generous helping of wisdom. Definitely pick it up.

CHAPTER 17
  1.) Check out this fascinating article on how Charles Dickens saved and shaped our modern Christmas: *http://mentalfloss.com/article/15531/how-charles-dickens-saved-christmas*

CHAPTER 22
  1.) From *The World According to Mister Rogers: Important Things to Remember* (2003) by Fred Rogers. I've said it before, no library is complete without Fred Rogers.

CHAPTER 25
  1.) Watch their full review on YouTube: *https://www.youtube.com/watchv=LmdqkFCUQcc*

~ A FEW ~
ACKNOWLEDGMENTS

In no particular order:

I would like to thank my friend **Cindy Larkey** for recommending *Olive, The Other Reindeer*. I don't think it's good exactly, but it was enjoyably bad and I'm glad I saw it! Thanks so much!

A special thanks to my friend **Brian Trumble** for his work on the cover. Thank you also for your help editing.

On the subject of the cover, I'd like to acknowledge artist **Norman Rockwell**. This cover is a tribute to his 1935 painting, "Christmas Santa Reading Mail," which served as a cover for the *Saturday Evening Post*. His work is largely to thank for informing our image of Santa and of Christmas, so do yourself a favor and go look up his stuff if you have not already. Many of his paintings (including this one) can be seen in the opening credits of *Ernest Saves Christmas*.

Thanks also to **Jodie Griggs**, both for another great author pic and also for driving us to the Keys and widening my musical horizons.

Thanks, **Justin Edwards**, for joining me to meet Pat Carroll and for helping with my car trouble that day.

Lastly, I cannot write a book about what Christmas means to me and not thank my parents, **Richard and Diane Korsiak**, for always making the holidays magical, for being the best Santa any kid could hope for, and for being Mrs. Claus when a certain stuffed dog needed a holiday miracle. I am a festive man thanks to the festive childhood you gave me. Thank you.

~ 25 ~
GREMLINS

"First of all, keep him out of the light, he hates bright light, especially sunlight, it'll kill him. Second, don't give him any water, not even to drink. But the most important rule, the rule you can never forget, no matter how much he cries, no matter how much he begs, never feed him after midnight."

Year: 1984
Distributor: Warner Bros.
Producer: Michael Finnell
Director: Joe Dante
Writer: Chris Columbus
Runtime: 82 minutes
Rating: PG

Scripture Reading: James 1:2-18

My favorite Christmas movie is *Gremlins.* I watch it every year with the same fervor that some people watch *A Christmas Story.* A struggling inventor discovers a strange creature called a Mogwai in a Chinese junk store. The owner, a wise old man, won't sell it, but the old man's grandson sneaks it to him in an alley behind the shop. The inventor wants to give it to his son Billy, an aspiring artist whose job at the bank supports the family. Gizmo, the Mogwai, comes with some very specific rules, and breaking them leads to the rise of a swarm of Gremlins.

The titular monsters of this film teach us a lesson in vice. The Gremlins are balls of manic destruction but can also be understood as metaphors for Sin. I'd even suggest that they represent the Seven Deadly Sins. Consider this: once the Gremlins have taken over Kingston Falls, what do they do? They gamble (Greed); they eat everything in sight (Gluttony); they "flash" Kate, the barmaid Billy is sweet on (Lust); they sabotage traffic lights and kill people (Wrath); they sing *their own movie's theme song* as a Christmas carol (Pride); they spitefully torture Gizmo (Envy); and they loaf around in bars and theaters instead of doing anything good or productive (Sloth).

And they are <u>adorable</u>!

Who's innocent in all of this? Gizmo, of course. He's the only "good" Mogwai. Technically, the bad ones all came from Gizmo, but they were only created because Billy didn't do his due diligence and follow the three rules:

1) No water, not even to drink.

2) No bright lights, especially sunshine.

3) No eating after midnight.

These rules are pretty straightforward, and it's worth noting that Billy didn't break any of them on purpose. Like most of us, his "sins" were just the result of a fundamental lack of vigilance. Billy knew that Gizmo wasn't supposed to get wet but let him have run of the bedroom, where the glass of water he used to wash his art brushes could spill.

Gizmo gets wet and the bad Mogwai pop out. Sin is born, just as our passage in James describes, but Sin wants to grow up. It's hungry, and only an after-midnight snack will do. Does Billy, having already shirked, double down on his efforts to be in control of the situation? Of course not! He lazily assumes that because his clock radio reads 11:40 that it's early enough and doesn't question it. Granted, any of us with a hungry, whiny cat could probably relate. Even so, he doesn't know what will happen if they eat after midnight. So far as Billy knows, eating after midnight could give them the sort of slow, painful death that Mrs. Deagle had in mind for Barney, the family dog. But no, rather than avoiding the risk by letting them go hungry, he feeds the Mogwai and offers food to Gizmo, who turns up his nose at the offer. Having eaten, the Mogwai metamorphose into Gremlins; the small sins become big ones - rampaging through town, murdering old ladies and Santa Clauses, and multiplying their way to the town movie theater to watch *Snow White*.

Kingston Falls is so Main Street USA that *The Blob* could have taken place there. It's the kind of neighborhood that our grandparents reminisce about when thinking of a simpler time that likely wasn't as good as they remember. It's *idyllic*. The town drunk is a harmless old veteran filled with stories about WWII. The town landlord is straight out of Capra's *It's a Wonderful Life* (which they will show you clips from in case you forget). Kingston Falls is paradise. But is it? Slowly, the veneer pulls away. We see a hungry family who Mrs. Deagle refuses to help. We learn with horror about how Kate discovered her father, pretending to be Santa, dead in a chimney. There are those who suggest that this scene is out of place, but it isn't. It's consistent with the tone of a movie which leads you behind the silver curtain, where at once you realize that what appears to be a screen of dancing, cartoon dwarfs on one side is a horde of ravening evil from a slightly different vantage point. And whether the shadows win or the dancing lights of our idealized youth depends not only on our choices, but the vigilance we exercise to maintain them.

Made in the USA
Columbia, SC
21 November 2017